THE TILE CLUB

AND THE AESTHETIC MOVEMENT IN AMERICA

THE TILE CLUB

AND THE AESTHETIC MOVEMENT IN AMERICA

BY RONALD G. PISANO

WITH ESSAYS BY MARY ANN APICELLA AND LINDA HENEFIELD SKALET

HARRY N. ABRAMS, INC., PUBLISHERS
IN ASSOCIATION WITH THE MUSEUMS AT STONY BROOK

This volume has been published in conjunction with the exhibition "The Tile Club and the Aesthetic Movement in America, 1877–1887."

Editor: Elaine M. Stainton
Designer: Judith Hudson

Exhibition Itinerary:

The Museums at Stony Brook
Stony Brook, New York
October 9, 1999–January 23, 2000

Lyman Allyn Art Museum
New London, Connecticut
February 5–May 7, 2000

The Frick Art Museum
Pittsburgh, Pennsylvania
May 19–August 13, 2000

Library of Congress Cataloging-in-Publication Data
Pisano, Ronald G.
   The Tile Club and the aesthetic movement in America / by
Ronald G. Pisano ; with essays by Mary Ann Apicella and
Linda Henefield Skalet.
        p.   cm.
Includes bibliographical references and index.
ISBN 0–8109–3894–4 (Abrams : cloth)
ISBN 0–8109–2933–3 (mus: pbk.)
1. Tile Club (New York, N.Y.) Exhibitions. 2. Decorative
arts—United States—History—19th century Exhibitions.
I. Apicella, Mary Ann. II. Skalet, Linda Henefield.
III. Title. IV. Title: Tile Club.
N6510.T53P47   1999
745'.0973'09034—dc21   99–28099

Pages 8 and 9: Tiles by Arthur Quartley and R. Swain Gifford.
Guild Hall Museum, East Hampton, New York

Printed and bound in Japan

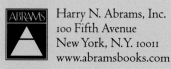 Harry N. Abrams, Inc.
100 Fifth Avenue
New York, N.Y. 10011
www.abramsbooks.com

 THE MUSEUMS
AT STONY BROOK

CONTENTS

Major funding for the publication
and the exhibition has been provided by:

The Henry Luce Foundation, Inc.

The New York State Council on the Arts

The Simons Foundation

The Cowles Charitable Trust

The Griffin

Winslow Homer. *Shepherdess Tile*. c. 1878.
Painted tile. 8 x 8". Lyman Allyn Museum,
New London, Connecticut

T C

DECORATIVE AGE OR DECORATIVE CRAZE?

THE ART AND ANTICS OF THE TILE CLUB (1877–1887)

By Ronald G. Pisano

In 1877, a year after the United States had celebrated its one-hundredth anniversary as a nation, and twelve years after the close of the Civil War, America embarked confidently on the journey into its second century. It was a period of consolidating wealth and a society noted for what the sociologist Thorstein Veblen would come to define as "conspicuous consumption."[1] The collecting of art, objets d'art, or anything else relatively expensive and serving little practical purpose became a means of signaling social status. New York City had become the art capital of the country, and the Hudson River School, with its romantic vision of America, had almost run its course. Gradually tastes were changing. In the fine arts, the dictates of these new standards were being established in the dominant European art centers of Paris and Munich, and those American artists returning from their studies in these cities might have expected a warm welcome. However, they found American collectors surprisingly

unsympathetic to their work, preferring, instead, the prestige that came with purchasing artwork produced by their European counterparts. This state of affairs was further complicated by the fact that the well established, and comparatively conservative, artists who governed the only major professional art organization and exhibition space in New York, the National Academy of Design, protected their domain against any serious infiltration by newcomers.

As a means of supplementing their income, American artists were obliged to take up teaching or illustrating. Teaching positions had opened up at the newly formed Art Students League (1875), and publishing firms, such as *Harper's* and *Scribner's*, hired illustrators. Still other fledgling artists turned to the decorative arts, responding to the collecting frenzy that had been sparked by the Centennial Exposition in Philadelphia in 1876 and fueled by the prosperity in post-Civil War America. Although America's presentation of decorative wares at the Centennial Exporition was comparatively paltry, those of other nations, particularly Great Britain, were both impressive and popular. The result was what has been termed the "Aesthetic Movement," a period which roughly spanned a decade from the mid-1870s to the mid-1880s and was characterized by an emphasis on handcrafted objects and paintings with a refined sense of design.[2] A wide range of magazines, such as the *Art Amateur* and *Art Interchange,* provided useful instruction to amateurs, while professional organizations like the Society of Decorative Arts (1877) were formed in New York and other large cities.

Many professional artists also turned their attention to decorative art, some almost exclusively. John Gardner Low, who founded the J. and J. G. Low Art Tile Works in Chelsea, Massachusetts, in 1877, capitalized on the growing popularity of ceramics and tiles following the Centennial Exposition. Two years later (1879), the painters Louis

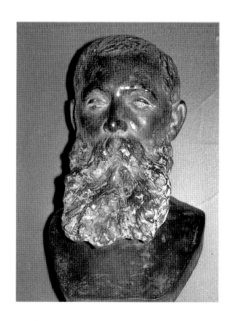

William O'Donovan. *Robert Swain Gifford.* 1879. Bronze. 23 x 10 ½ x 10". The Century Association, New York

William O'Donovan. *Ye Tile Manne (Edwin Austin Abbey).* 1878. Clay. Yale University, New Haven, Connecticut

Image taken from "The Tile Club at Play," Scribner's Monthly, *Vol. XVII, No. 4, p. 465*

Comfort Tiffany, Samuel Colman, Lockwood de Forest, and Candace Wheeler joined forces to establish the interior design firm, Associated Artists.

In order to promote their own artwork, which remained outside the decorative realm, and to circumvent the limiting exhibition policies of the National Academy of Design, in 1878 a number of young artists formed the Society of American Artists in New York. Fraternal organizations, such as the Salmagundi Sketch Club established in 1877 (an outgrowth of a sketch club formed in 1871), provided an informal forum for artists to vent their frustrations, commiserate with one another over financial problems, discuss the latest developments in art, and socialize.[3] Among the several other notable art clubs that were started around this time was the Tile Club — perhaps the smallest, one of the shortest lived, and most definitely the least understood.

The details regarding the formation, activities, and raison d'être of the Tile Club are veiled in obscurity, calculated by its members to create an air of exclusivity and attract attention. Basic information can only be gleaned from careful reading of the several contemporary articles published about the group — accounts written and illustrated by club members — which can seldom, if ever, be taken at face value. Each article supplied to the press was a carefully crafted conundrum filled with personal jokes and code names and embroidered with descriptions of activities devised both to confound and amuse the cognoscenti of the art world and the general public. Those "in the know" could decipher the innuendos, puns, and satirical remarks, while the average reader who could not still managed to follow an entertaining story line, accompanied by charming illustrations.

J. Alden Weir. *Self Portrait.* 1886. Oil on canvas. 21 x 17¼". National Academy of Design, New York

Napoleon Sarony. *F. Hopkinson Smith.* c. 1880. Crayon on paper. 14½ x 10". The New-York Historical Society, New York

The first article published about the Tile Club, written by club member William Mackay Laffan, appeared as "The Tile Club at Work," in *Scribner's Monthly* (January 1879).[4] This account, which included fifteen illustrations (two-thirds of which were of tiles or were tile-related) served to introduce the group to the public. The Tile Club was established in the fall of 1877 by a group of young artists and writers living in New York City who met informally in each other's studios to discuss matters of art. Although there is no record of "charter members," among the earliest to join were two Englishmen recently transplanted in the United States — Walter Paris (a painter) and Edward Wimbridge (an architect); several illustrators — Edwin Austin Abbey, Charles S. Reinhart, and Winslow Homer (who was also an established artist at this point); two painters of land and sea — Arthur Quartley and R. Swain Gifford; one sculptor — William O'Donovan; two

DECORATIVE AGE OR DECORATIVE CRAZE

newspaper writers — Earl Shinn (who usually wrote under the name Edward Strahan) and William Mackay Laffan; and one "jack of all trades" – F. Hopkinson Smith (illustrator, painter, writer, and engineer).[5] A suggestion was made to form a club that would relate not only to their professions, but would reflect the prevailing mode of taste in America, which was for decorative objects and paintings, preferably based on European standards, as prompted by the Centennial Exposition.

It was a time, one of them later recalled, when "decorative mania . . . had fallen like a destructive angel upon the most flourishing cities in America, turning orderly homes into bristling and impenetrable curiosity-shops."[6] The overwhelming popularity of decorative objects actually had an adverse affect on the sale of paintings (or at least those that did not conform to the aesthetics of this movement). Responding to this situation one of the artists suggested their new club be based on some sort of decorative notion so that they would not be "behind the times."[7] Another scoffed at the idea, declaring that he would not lower his standards; he then assured the others, "It is only a temporary craze, a phase of popular insanity that will wear itself out as soon as a new hobby is presented to take its place."[8] Someone else countered that the current interest in decorative pursuits was "encouraging evidence of the growing influence of our methods of art education."[9] And yet another maintained it was indeed an obligation on their part as professional artists to set an example in the decorative arts to prevent the "uncultivated" from proceeding "blindly to ridiculous extremes."[10] It is difficult to ascertain just how much of this repartee is genuine and how much is tongue-in-cheek. In any event, one enthusiastic artist proclaimed, "Let us be decorative!"[11] And, evidently, there was no further opposition.

Just what form of decorative art should they pursue? Suggestions included fresco, wallpaper, and fabric design, most certainly options inspired by the popularity of the English designers William Morris and Charles Locke

Eastlake, or even the painter Lawrence Alma-Tadema. Their celebrity was underscored by Great Britain's strong presence at the Centennial Exposition, described by Abbey to be "by far the most interesting" in the show.[12] London-born Walter Paris agreed, as did the English architect Edward Wimbridge, who finally came up with the "winning" idea: tiles. "Tiles are what we need," Wimbridge declared. "The element of color and variety is lost in the decorative details of our structures."[13] A skeptic in the ranks queried, ". . . and when you've done them, what'll you do with them?"[14] "Why, just what you do with the pictures you paint," answered another, "[you] keep them" – no doubt a reference to the pitiful sale of their paintings.[15] Wimbridge pointed out the many uses for tiles put forth by "our English neighbors," and with no further delay, the group moved on to other issues.[16]

The fraternal nature of the association was paramount, as was the value of "comparing notes about the results of summer work out-of-doors."[17] It was stressed that unlike other city clubs, theirs must be informal, with no bylaws, officers, initiation fees, or dues. In order to insure exclusivity, membership was limited to twelve; in line with affecting a "studiously slangy and Bohemian" air, each member would be assigned a sobriquet humorously reflecting some aspect of his physical character, personality, artistic temperament, or some play on words.[18] For instance, Laffan was named "Polyphemus" after the one-eyed mythological creature because he had only one good eye (the other being glass); and Quartley, almost exclusively a painter of the sea, was named the "Marine." These club names were always used in their publications to stress the select nature of the group, as well as to create a sense of intrigue and inject an element of humor.[19] (See appendix for a complete list of Tile Club sobriquets.)

Meetings of the Tile Club were held each Wednesday evening at the studios of artist members on a rotating basis. The first was at the studio of Walter Paris at 3 Union Square; Wimbridge was the only other member to show

Edward Wimbridge. *A Tile Man's Design*. 1878.
Dimensions unknown. Image taken from
"The Tile Club at Work," *Scribner's Monthly*,
January 1879, Vol. XVII, No. 3, p. 407

up.[20] The evening "tile painting exercise" proved to be so unsuccessful that the two relieved their frustration by purportedly throwing their pitiful productions at each other.[21] Abbey and Reinhart attended the second meeting and subsequently were joined by Homer, O'Donovan, Laffan, Quartley, Gifford, Shinn, Smith, and the painter J. Alden Weir, who was inducted into the club in April of 1878.

None of the artists is known to have had any previous experience in the field of tile painting, but with further effort, much to their surprise, "a certain fascination was found in these experiments."[22] Little is known about the technical aspects of their early exploits. Although tiles of a "Spanish make," cream-white in color, were originally designated to be used, all the extant tiles examined thus far are stamped either by "Josiah Wedgwood" or "Minton Stoke on Trent." These English ceramic manufacturers provided blank "bisquited wares," ready for decorating and glaze-firing in studio kilns, to the amateur market. Both the Wedgwood and Minton tiles were cream-white in color and 8 x 8 inches square, the type and shape prescribed by the group.[23] The medium used was identified variously as "German inks," "mineral colors," and ultimately "tubes of vitreous paints invented by Lacroix."[24] Application of the medium had to be done swiftly and unfalteringly, as the porous surface quickly absorbed the pigment. As club members began to master the technique, they enjoyed experimenting with the process further: one rubbed bitumen over his tile; another employed the tip of a wooden match to scratch out highlights; while a third, who used his thumbs to create atmospheric effects, discovered the technique had a "hit-or-miss" element similar to using a palette knife.[25] The result was a luminous quality superior to that which could be achieved in oil painting on canvas. "I believe I am getting the pearly shadows on flesh to-day," declared one Tiler, "and it is a tile that is teaching me."[26] Another gleefully announced that he was creating a "regular Constable tempest in a teapot."[27]

William Merritt Chase. *Bearded Man Wearing*
a Flat Hat. c. 1879. Painted and glazed tile.
8 x 8". Private collection

William Merritt Chase. *The Musketeer.*
c. 1879. Painted and glazed tile. 9⅞ x 9".
Private collection

DECORATIVE AGE OR DECORATIVE CRAZE
—

R. Swain Gifford. *Figure in Tree*. 1879. Painted
and glazed earthenware. 8 x 8". Collection
Graham D. Williford

R. Swain Gifford. *Untitled.* 1879. Painted
and glazed earthenware. 8 x 8". Collection
Graham D. Williford

Arthur Quartley. *Rocky Shore*. 1879. Painted
and glazed tile. 8 x 8". Private collection

Walter Paris. *Sprig of Leaves.* 1879. Painted
and glazed earthenware. 8 x 8". Guild
Hall Museum, East Hampton, New York.
Gift of the David Tyson Foundation,
Carolyn Tyson and Edith Frankel, supple-
mented by the Guild Hall Purchase Fund

DECORATIVE AGE OR DECORATIVE CRAZE
—

Charles S. Reinhart. *Untitled*. c. 1879. Painted and glazed earthenware. 8 x 8". Guild Hall Museum, East Hampton, New York. Gift of the David Tyson Foundation, Carolyn Tyson and Edith Frankel, supplemented by the Guild Hall Purchase Fund

Frederick Dielman. *Kine Tile*. c. 1879. Painted and glazed tile. 8 x 8". Private collection

Frederick Dielman. *Untitled.* c. 1879. Painted
and glazed earthenware. 8 x 8". Guild Hall
Museum, East Hampton, New York. Gift of
the David Tyson Foundation, Carolyn Tyson
and Edith Frankel, supplemented by the
Guild Hall Purchase Fund

*This tile is said to have been started by Edwin
Austin Abbey.*

Soon a routine developed. No subjects or themes were
dictated, and the results were wide-ranging: landscapes,
seascapes, figures, portraits, and florals. A long table was
provided (or improvised) in the middle of the room,
on which the evening's host arranged tiles, small palettes,
turpentine, brushes of various sizes, pencils, rags, color
tubes, and "student lamps." Everyone was in his place by
half past eight, "cleaning off his tile with 'turps' and a rag,
or sketching in his design with a lead-pencil or a bit of
lithographic crayon."[28] It should be noted that O'Donovan,
the only sculptor when the club was founded, produced
unpainted bas-relief tiles modeled in clay or wax, and cast
in plaster. Some members painted directly without any
underdrawing, while others first drew their design on the
tile and then painted. Often many attempts were made
and obliterated before a satisfactory design was achieved.
Those times when no successful tile was completed,
the Tiler would finish his work at home. Nearly all the

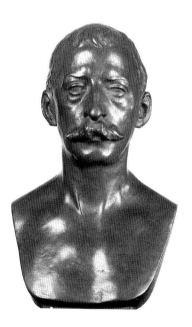

Winslow Homer. *Resting Shepherdess*. 1878.
Painted and glazed tiles. 8 x 16". Collection
Karen H. Bechtel

tiles were monochromatic or had a limited color range,
"Victoria blue" and brown being the most favored colors.
This was attributed to the fact that work was done at
night by lamplight, which made it difficult to attain natural color effects.[29] The exception to this rule was Winslow
Homer, who in several of his tiles used a wide array of
brilliant colors as evidenced in his double tile, *Resting
Shepherdess*. Aside from this work's impressive range of color,
its detail, modeling, and attention paid to atmospheric
effects suggest strongly that it was done in Homer's studio,
in daylight, and was based on plein-air studies. Related
sketches by Homer substantiate this theory.[30]

Homer was clearly one of the most adventurous of the
Tile Club members. Aside from being daring with regard
to color, he was prolific, completing at least six known
single tiles, one plaque, and two elaborate fireplace sur-
rounds (the only ones known to have been completed by

Winslow Homer. *Fireplace Tiles*. 1878.
Ceramic tiles, each 8 x 8". Private collection

a single member of the club).[31] One of these fire sur-rounds, dated 1878, is made up of three 8 x 8-inch tiles depicting dolphinlike sea creatures arranged vertically on either side, while across the top is a frieze of three tiles, on which a beach scene with two women is painted. This image relates to Homer's painting *Promenade on the Beach*, 1880. The second and more ambitious fireplace surround, *Pastoral*, includes monumentally conceived images of a shepherd on the left and shepherdess on the right, each extending over three 8 x 8-inch tiles. The frieze across the top (extending between the heads of the two figures) depicts a cloudy sky and the top of a hill. Although said to have been done for his brother, Charles Savage Homer, Jr., or at least destined for his home, it is inscribed "Copy-right, 1878, by Winslow Homer," suggesting the artist might have considered pursuing some sort of commercial venture along this line; however, no such endeavor has since been documented.[32]

Apparently Homer was pleased with his tile making, exhibiting his wares at the Century Club and at a private

viewing for friends and patrons in his studio. His studio also served as the setting for the club's first "annual" din-ner, held in the spring of 1878, at which time the idea of a summer sketching trip, "a journey in search of the pic-turesque," was suggested by F. Hopkinson Smith.[33] The idea was enthusiastically received. Abbey proposed a trip to the Catskills, while Gifford suggested the Adirondacks, and Quartley favored the Isles of Shoals. Reinhart offered for consideration the coast of Maine, and Laffan, passen-ger agent for the Long Island Railroad (and responsible for promoting tourism) quite naturally proposed Long Island. "That sandy place?" questioned Paris. "There's nothing there," added Shinn.[34] Furthermore, "Nobody was ever known to go there!" Wimbridge complained.[35] This last comment spurred the curiosity of Smith, who exclaimed, "Nobody ever went there! Then that's the place of all others to go to!"[36] This repartee demonstrates how much of the Tile Club's stories must have been improvised for the sake of entertainment. Clearly Homer had visited eastern Long Island as early as 1874, when he painted on

Winslow Homer. *Promonade on the Beach.*
1880. Oil on canvas. 20 x 30½". Springfield
Museum of Fine Arts, Springfield,
Massachusetts

DECORATIVE AGE OR DECORATIVE CRAZE

the beach in East Hampton, yet this was completely ignored.[37] In any event, Reinhart suggested that they might sell the account of their excursion to some "grasping publisher."[38] While both newspapermen in the group were reported to have some doubts about that possibility, the trip took place the summer of 1878 and a chronicle of the journey would appear in *Scribner's Monthly* the following winter (February 1879) as "The Tile Club at Play."[39]

On June 10, 1878, eleven members of the Tile Club, "animated by a spirit of decoration," met at the western terminus of the Long Island Railroad, Hunter's Point, to begin their venture. Attending were: O'Donovan, Laffan, Gifford, Paris, Abbey, Reinhart, Smith, Quartley, Wimbridge, Shinn, and William Baird, a well known baritone singer who had been newly elected honorary musician member.[40] As this was the club's first trip, the members dressed "incongruously," and were very conspicuous with their cumbersome painting gear. Amused by the sight, O'Donovan described the group as having "a very tiley

appearance."[41] Laffan, as a railroad employee (and conduit for free passage), was quite naturally their guide as they boarded the train en route to Babylon, where they would catch a boat to Captree Island, off Long Island's south shore. Braced against inclement weather and buoyed by high spirits, the club managed to engage the services of the sloop *Amelia Corning* to deliver them to "Castle Conklin," an ironic name for a hodgepodge of connected clapboard structures overseen by its proprietor, Uncle Jesse Conklin. At sunrise, the industrious Gifford was among the first "out hunting for a sketch," which he titled *Morning at Jesse Conklin's.*[42] As the weather cleared, the others appeared, "intent and studious persons, bending assiduously over [watercolor] blocks or sketch-books; some seated in chairs; others on the backs of them; some on sketching stools; others on boxes or in holes in the sand."[43]

By early afternoon, the artists left for Lake Ronkonkoma via Sayville, where they purchased enormous straw hats to shade them from the sun as they set off on their six-mile walk behind a horse-drawn wagon engaged to carry their luggage; a humorous rendition of the weary entourage was captured by Abbey in his drawing *Procession of Ye Tilers*. Although arriving exhausted and barely in time for dinner at Mrs. Carpenter's hotel, the travelers managed to find the energy to take a nighttime cruise on beautiful Lake Ronkonkoma. Reinvigorated, the next day the group continued their journey by stagecoach and rail to Bridge-hampton, where the artists made sketches of the windmill and local inhabitants. Smith discovered a milliner's shop and convinced the others to adorn their straw hats with colorful ribbons, an event dutifully recorded by Reinhart in *The Tile Club and the Milliner of Bridgehampton*, a sort of traveler's memento.

Without further delay (they had actually covered considerable ground in just two and one-half days), the group proceeded to East Hampton, the main destination of their pilgrimage, where they began sketching the wealth of picturesque material before them. The range of their work reveals that they were clearly not representative of any specific school of art. Paris began working in a style of "severe minuteness, in the pre-Raphaelite way," but as night descended, and detail became blurred, he was forced to shift his approach, finishing his painting with a "few smeary daubs, declaring himself an impressionist."[44] Abbey attempted a windmill "in colors," but the dramatic effect of its "apparitional wings" eluded him.[45] Reinhart produced a "Nocturne in black and blue," obviously a pun on the titles

R. Swain Gifford. *Morning at Jesse Conklin's.*
1878. Watercolor and gouache on paper.
3⅝ x 6⅝". Private collection

Charles S. Reinhart. *The Tile Club and the Milliner of Bridgehampton.* 1878. Mixed media on paper. 18 x 24". Prints Division, New York Public Library

Standing (left to right): Earl Shinn, F. Hopkinson Smith, Charles S. Reinhart, Walter Paris, Edward Wimbridge, William O'Donovan, William Baird, Arthur Quartley. Seated (left to right): Edwin A. Abbey, R. Swain Gifford, William Laffan.

Edwin Austin Abbey. *Procession of Ye Tilers.*
1878. Ink on cardboard. 4½ x 22⅛".
Collection Graham D. Williford

Arthur Quartley. *Girl on Beach, East Hampton.*
1878. Painted and glazed tile. 8 x 8". East
Hampton Free Library, East Hampton,
New York

James McNeill Whistler gave his tonal paintings of the
1860s; and Quartley created a "Hallucination in purple and
prisms," perhaps a humorous allusion to Impressionism.[46]

The artists found East Hampton to be a veritable
"painter's gold-mine, all bits and nuggets," which they celebrated in their many on-the-spot sketches.[47] Their activity
as plein-air painters (an experience new to most of them)
is delightfully captured in Abbey's painting en grisaille,
Sketching at East Hampton, in which he portrayed his colleagues
Quartley and Smith in a carefree moment of painting
directly outdoors shielded from the harsh sun by umbrellas.
However, the main purpose in visiting East Hampton was
to "guy," or mock, the local celebrity John Howard Payne.
Author of the tremendously popular song *Home Sweet Home*,
which was said to have been inspired by his hometown
of East Hampton, Payne was then living in England. After
listening to endless tales of Payne's early youth and visiting several cottages where he was said to have been born,
the artists went back to painting.

It is not clear how long the Tilers stayed in East
Hampton – probably several days – before continuing
on to Montauk. Before leaving, however, they entertained
local villagers with their own musical rendition of *Home
Sweet Home*. They reached Montauk by carriages, com-
menting along the way about local history, including the
"once valorous Montauk tribe . . . reduced to a pitiful
handful."[48] At Montauk they visited "King" David
Pharaoh, who had asserted himself as sachem of all living
Long Island Indians. When one of the Tilers asked to
sketch him, Pharaoh declared, "I wouldn't like to. There
was an insulting sketch of me made some time ago."[49]
This was probably another apocryphal yarn devised by
the Tilers as an oblique reference to Winslow Homer, who
had made a sketch of Pharaoh in 1874.[50] It also further
suggests that Homer might have influenced the groups'
choice of sights to visit on Long Island. From Montauk
they began their journey home, stopping at a fashionable
hotel on Shelter Island, where they "resumed the habits

Edwin Austin Abbey. *Sketching at East Hampton.* 1878. Ink and Chinese white on paper. 11 x 17". Private collection

Anonymous. *Members of the Tile Club Sketching, Greenport.* 1878. Photograph. Lightfoot Collection

of civilization . . . [and were] reabsorbed into the relentless tide of commonplace".[51] A photograph identified "members of the Tile Club sketching, Greenport," dated 1878, suggests they stopped on the "north fork" on their trip back to New York.

Close on the heels of the *Scribner's Monthly* article (February 1879) which included twenty-seven illustrations (only five of which seem to be designs for tiles), there appeared a booklet produced by Laffan for the Long Island Railroad, *The New Long Island: A Handbook of Summer Travel.*[52] Much of the text and many of the illustrations were derived from the magazine account of the Tilers' trip. The purpose of this publication was clearly promotional, and the artwork was used as endorsements for tourism on Long Island. Fares to every village were included, and as an inducement to settle on Long Island, the railroad offered one year of free travel to newcomers, obviously a means of increasing ridership.

During the winter of 1878–79, the composition of the Tile Club began to change, as did its focus. Two of its earliest members, and avid supporters of painting tiles, Wimbridge and Paris, left, the first for Bombay, the second for a remote island in the English Channel. The club's staunchest Anglophile (also a great admirer of English crafts), Abbey, moved to London. New inductees included the painters William Merritt Chase, John H. Twachtman, Frederick Dielman, and the lithographer and fashionable photographer Napoleon Sarony. The club still met on Wednesday evenings; and although artist members continued to paint tiles, interest in this pursuit was already beginning to wane.

Meanwhile, the Tilers discussed plans for their summer trip of 1879. One proposed that they "hire a schooner, and explore the Long Island Sound, in search of literary and artistic remains; but the undulating character of the Sound waters caused the idea to be rejected."[53] Another suggested the New Jersey shore, but this was turned down because of its preponderance of mosquitos. O'Donovan

J. Alden Weir. *Portrait of John H. Twachtman.* c. 1894. Oil on canvas. 21½ x 17¾". Cincinnati Art Museum

William Merritt Chase and Frank Duveneck. *Portrait of Frederick Dielman.* 1882. Oil on canvas. 30 x 24⅞". National Academy of Design, New York

Anonymous. *Interior of the Tile Club Barge.* 1879. Archives of American Art, Washington, D.C.

then "feebly" advanced the idea of a canal voyage, but got no response. Several meetings later Smith reintroduced O'Donovan's proposal with more detail (and perhaps more vigor), and the group became intrigued with the thought of hiring a boat to travel up the Hudson River, through the Erie Canal to Lake Champlain. It was decided: upstate New York it would be. The activities of the Tilers during this summer trip were fully recorded and illustrated in an article for *Scribner's Monthly* the following March (1880) under the title "The Tile Club Afloat." The account consisted of thirty-one pages and thirty-nine illustrations, none of which can positively identified as tiles or designs for tiles.[54]

After many days of effort seeking a clean barge, the *John C. Earle* was finally engaged for twenty days at seven dollars a day. It was lavishly decorated by the "Committee on Decoration and Home Comforts," with artistic trappings gleaned from the elaborate studios of Chase and Sarony. As one might imagine, "the artistic and decorative effect that was produced was excellent. . . . The divans,

that were easily translated into beds; the cushions, that were but pretexts for diurnal concealment of pillows; the piano, the violins, the big dining table, the armchairs and hammocks, the excellent glassware . . . cutlery . . . student lamps and Chinese lanterns" were all serviceable and, of course, tastefully selected.[55] The "major domo and brush-washer" of this deluxe affair, a black servant named Daniel, was bedecked with a "snowy linen cap and jacket and a long white apron."[56] Assisting him was a second servant whom the Tilers named "Deuteronomy." It is no wonder that all but two of the members showed up at the pier at West Tenth Street on the morning of June 23, 1879, to partake of this luxury cruise presumably at the expense of *Scribner's.* Tilers who made up the 1879 expedition included O'Donovan, Laffan, Gifford, Reinhart, Smith, Quartley, Dielman, Chase, Sarony, Weir, Twachtman, Baird, Dr. J. Lewenberg (who played the violin), Antonio Knauth (who played the cello), and Gustave Kobbé (a publisher, music critic and pianist), the last three having been, along with Baird, elected honorary musician members of the club. The only members missing were Shinn and Homer. Homer had probably dropped out of the club by this time. From this point on, it is difficult to keep an exact count of Tile Club members. It does appear, however, that an effort was made to keep the core group at twelve.

The barge was hitched to a "community" of forty-two boats being pulled and pushed up the Hudson by tug boats. Five days later, Gifford wrote to his wife Fanny that they were moving at a "snail's pace" and were just arriving in Albany, but wasted no time in beginning sketches: "Yesterday morning was very pleasant and we made a number of sketches on the different boats, going from one to the other by means of a plank put across from one gunwale to the other."[57] Much to the amusement of passengers on the other boats, the artists dressed in "gorgeous costumes."[58] They also had a large Japanese bell, three feet high, which they struck at mealtime and "when any remarkable vessel passed by."[59]

To while away the time on their slow river journey, the artists quite appropriately discussed the Hudson River School of art, its members, and their "good old mossy, geographical landscapes which used to crowd the holy precincts of the National Academy," by this point considered passé.[60] In contrasting the visions of "grandeur and sublimity," as represented in the landscapes of the previous generation to the recent work of the Tilers and their colleagues, Gifford observed: "Simplicity alone has evaded us all along."[61]

At Albany, the Tilers' barge was separated from the community of boats and the contingent set off "at a comparatively tremendous rate of speed," guided by a single tug as seen in Quartley's illustration, *Parting Company with the Tow, West Troy*.[62] At West Troy they took on yet another servant, whom they dubbed "Priam," after the last king of ancient Troy. The image of this stately individual, described by the group as being "a prepossessing young man . . . [with] qualities of mind and person that were

William Merritt Chase. *Self Portrait*. c. 1879. Pencil on paper. 15¼ x 11⅞". Private collection

John H. Twachtman. *New York Harbor.* 1879.
Oil on canvas. 10½ x 12". Courtesy Cooley
Gallery, Old Lyme, Connecticut

R. Swain Gifford. *Hudson River Tow*. 1879.
Etching. 7 x 8 ¹⁵⁄₁₆". Whaling Museum,
New Bedford, Massachusetts

Arthur Quartley. *Parting Company with the Tow,
West Troy*. 1879. Oil on board. 9 x 12¼".
Private collection

not unworthy of the distinguished name he bore," was recorded for posterity by Chase in his *Priam, the Nubian Ganymede.*[63] It was at West Troy "from amongst the crowds of roustabouts in leather aprons, and small boys fringing the string-pieces of wharves with bare and muddy legs, that little Jessie Miller emerged, like sun from vapor."[64] Invited on board to play the piano, she "pursued the thread of her melody" that at first "astonished discords" in the sensitive instrument, "accustomed hitherto to Chopin and Beethoven . . . [which] then bleated obediently."[65] This charming image of the diminutive girl's delightful performance was captured in Dielman's drawing, *Jessie Miller.* Upon leaving West Troy, the barge entered the Northern Canal and was attached to a team of mules, whereupon the Tilers experienced the "true poetry of motion that the humble and misunderstood tow-path confers."[66] The next day they tied up at Weaver's Basin, where some of the artists went ashore to paint the bucolic landscape, and Weir painted a portrait of Quartley, *The Marine*, showing him wearing the big straw hat he had acquired on the summer trip to Long Island in 1878.

J. Alden Weir. *The Marine (Portrait of Arthur Quartley)*. 1879. Oil on canvas. 18 x 12".
Private collection

Frederick Dielman. *Jessie Miller (The Little Trojan)*. 1879. Pencil on paper. 6 ¼ x 4 ½".
Private collection

The Tilers celebrated the Fourth of July in Schuyler-ville, where the mayor turned out to pay them the honor of a visit, as did local residents who delighted in trying on various costumes including a mandarin's crape robe, Mongolian pagoda hats, and Frans Hals ruffs. In honor of the holiday, the Tilers visited local sights dating back to Colonial times, being transported about in carriages provided by the town fathers, "each of which had thought-fully been furnished with . . . an elderly and communica-tive native," who supplied more than adequate details.[67] The artists then continued along the Northern Canal where they were greeted with gifts of flowers and fruits and, in turn, invited the locals aboard their floating museum and curiosity shop. They then proceeded to Whitehall, where a little cutter was placed at their disposal to sail on Lake Champlain, touching upon the shore of Vermont before returning for the trip home on July 9. At Whitehall they met the daughter of Parson William Miller (1782–1849), a minister who had mistakenly declared the end of the world and the coming of Christ would occur in 1843. "The ancient dame moved with difficulty down the padded stairs. . . . Then, to the astonishment of everyone . . . she noticed the cello . . . And soon she was actually tuning and managing the instrument, playing and singing 'Come to the sunset tree' and other lyrics of a long-gone time."[68] Along the way, they had the opportunity of actually visit-ing a tileworks, where ". . . as tilers should [they] made themselves at home. The kiln, the mill that ground the clay, the heaps of tubes like crimson macaroni, the boy that minded the fire, all were food for artistic reflec-tion."[69] Gifford documented the visit in a sketch, *The Tile Bakery* (location unknown).[70]

The return trip down the Hudson was described as "pure delight."[71] Little detail is provided except that the same crew of the boats in their tow up the river accompa-nied them on their voyage home; all of them brought their friends to see the "wonders of the sailing studio."[72] After twenty days of cruising, their journey came to an

Charles S. Reinhart. *Come to the Sunset Tree.*
1879. Pen and ink on paper. 7½ x 3¾".
Private collection

end: "The era of uneasiness, of bag strapping, of little casual goodbyes, was come."[73] The group disembarked at the wharf in New York City and returned to their studios.

Among the guests the Tile Club hosted later that year was the expatriate artist Elihu Vedder, recently returned from Italy for a visit. On December 3, 1879, he was invited to a meeting and introduced to each Tiler by the gregarious Chase.[74] Apparently Vedder was somewhat intimidated by the experience, although he joined the others in painting (a work on canvas rather than a tile). In spite of Vedder's apprehension, Smith implored him to visit again. When he returned on December 11, he met another guest, Robert Underwood Johnson of *Scribner's*, who mentioned that his magazine planned to do an article on him.[75] Vedder, who was older than most of the Tilers, had strong ties

with the "old guard" at the National Academy of Design, but was delighted by the attention he received from the Tilers, writing home to his wife, "The old fellows consider I belong to them, so do the young."[76]

On January 31, 1880, shortly before *Scribner's Monthly* released its article on the Tile Club's summer trip of 1879, *Harper's Weekly* published a general "update" on the club, written by Laffan.[77] Included with the text was an illustration by Reinhart showing a club meeting at the luxurious studio of one of its recently joined members, Sarony. Thirteen men are gathered around the table, along with five musicians grouped near the piano. Although it was still maintained that club membership was limited to twelve, guests often attended the meetings, and those who were artists almost "always sat down and contributed a plaque

William Merritt Chase. *Woman on a Shore.*
c. 1880. Painted porcelain plate. 9" diameter.
Baker/Pisano Collection

Charles S. Reinhart. *Tile Club Meeting.*
Published in *Harper's Weekly*, January 31, 1880,
Vol. XXIV, no. 1205, pp. 72–73

*Members that can be identified in Reinhart's (center)
illustration include (at left) F. Hopkinson Smith (standing), Frederick Dielman seated to his right, Napoleon
Sarony holding up what appears to be a tile seated to
his left, Charles Reinhart (the next standing figure)
with William Merritt Chase seated to his right, and
R. Swain Gifford seated to his left. In the right corner,
the figure holding the violin is possibly Dr. Lewenberg,
with Antonio Knauth playing the cello and Gustave
Kobbé on the piano. The tiles and plaques surrounding
the center illustration are by (starting at the lower
left): Sarony, Smith, Shinn, Quartley, Weir, Dielman,
Laffan, Reinhart, Gifford, another by Gifford,
another by Gifford, and the last by Chase. The three
drawings on the bottom of the page (the landscapes
titled "Long Island," "Northern Canal," and the still
life in between) are not signed.*

Arthur Quartley. *Steamboat Near a Shore.*
1879. Painted and glazed tile. 8 x 8". Private
collection

William O'Donovan. *Alice Gerson*. 1884.
Plaster. 7 ⅗ x 5 ⅗ x ⅗ ". Pennsylvania
Academy of the Fine Arts, Philadelphia.
Gift of Mrs. Talcott Williams

for the benefit of the host of the evening."[78] Surrounding the image of the group is a beautifully decorated border incorporating eight tiles and three plaques. At the lower corners appear commemorative scenes of the Tilers' two summer trips, inscribed "Long Island" and "Northern Canal," connected by a still life of sketching gear. Among the images that can be identified are tiles by Quartley, Weir, Laffan, Reinhart, Gifford, Chase, Sarony, and Smith; and plaques by Shinn, Dielman, and Gifford. In a sense, this article marked their "last hurrah" as tile painters, "a decorative craze that took possession of a number of otherwise worthy artists," as its author explained.[79] By the summer of 1879, they had come to realize that every member was "heavily long of keramics," and it was highly suspected that even their good-natured friends had received more than their fair share of "peculiar presents."[80] In response to this "plethora of tiles," they decided to move on to round plaques, which provided, temporarily at least, a different shape.

The next major account of the Tile Club's activities did not appear until February of 1882, when "The Tile Club Ashore" was published in *The Century Magazine*, consisting of eighteen pages and twenty illustrations, none of which were of tiles.[81] This article offered some insight as to what had happened to the group over the previous two years, however, its explanation cannot be taken at face value. The excuse given for the delay of the article's appearance was "the unostentatious practices and modest habits of that worthy body have led it to avoid the public gaze and to prefer the seclusive charm to be found with itself alone."[82] In reality, the club delighted in publicity, while continually reinforcing its exclusivity. A more reasonable explanation is that the artists were busy with other matters, and it had taken them this long to gather enough material to piece together an interesting, although relatively brief, article. Laffan, the author, reiterated the growing tendency of the group to depart from the original purpose of painting tiles. Now any artistic pursuit

William O'Donovan. *Virginia Gerson*. 1881.
Plaster. 10 ¼ x 7 ½". Collection Graham D.
Williford

was permissible, as the Wednesday night worktable was
"covered with drawing-boards, blocks of water-color
paper, small canvasses, charcoal and pencil paper, tiles and
plaques; and brushes, paints, 'turps' and materials of all
kinds."[83] O'Donovan continued to do plaster bas reliefs,
including two images of the Gerson sisters, Alice and
Virginia, who posed as models for members of the group.
Later Alice became Chase's wife. A current breakdown of
documented tiles confirms the dramatic decline in their
production by this point: of the forty-seven datable tiles/
plaques, 96 percent were done between 1878 and 1879.

As early as 1882, in an attempt to explain the scarcity
of tiles, Laffan claimed that most had been destroyed
when the warehouse in which they were stored burned
down. He then facetiously reported that "the public and
the press deplored for weeks the irreparable loss of so
priceless an accumulation of objects of art."[84] In contrast,
Smith considered the check that he anticipated from the
insurance company to be a "dispensation of Providence!"[85]
This is more likely just another of the club's fabricated
stories, since the artists constantly complained they had
trouble paying studio rent, much less paying storage
space for tiles. More plausibly, the production of tiles
was modest, a fact they were embarrassed to acknowledge.

Although the focus of the club had been diverted
from the painting of tiles, Laffan assured his readers that
the "spirit . . . remains the same."[86] Indeed, the Tile Club
had evolved basically into a social organization, with a
certain cachet about town based, in part, on its restrictive
membership policy. As such, it still afforded its members
a forum for the discussion of art matters, especially issues
relating to plein-air painting stemming from their summer sketching trips.

The Tilers' last trip, another excursion to Long Island,
described in *The Century Magazine* article of 1882 was in fact,
an amalgamation of two trips, one in the summer of 1880
and another in the fall of 1881.[87] The account begins with
the planning of what would become the trip in 1880. It was

reported that "one-half of the members would be satisfied with nothing short of an ocean voyage."[88] However, many were too pressed for funds, including O'Donovan, who intended to "retire to a wind-swept beach" on Long Island and set up quarters in the remains of a wrecked ship, *The Two Sisters*.[89] He proceeded to tell the story of the schooner, which lay just fifty miles by boat from New York City, and of his plans to live in its hulk. Dielman and Shinn, intrigued by the artistic prospects and piqued by the romantic notion, expressed interest in joining O'Donovan, and gradually so did the others. Just how much of the story that follows is true is unknown. There was, indeed, a schooner named *The Two Sisters* (from Greenport, Long Island) that was struck by the steamship *Massachusetts* (from Providence, Rhode Island) in the Long Island Sound between Captain's Island and Sands Point on July 17, 1877.[90] Either its wreck was their true destination, or the fact of its existence became the basis for elaboration. In either case, the 1880 trip was likely made to this general area on Long Island's north shore. The trip was scheduled for June, at which point those planning to go met at West Tenth Street to board the *P.B Casket*, property of T. J. Coffin, Esq., names that appear to be puns improvised as an element of ominous humor for what was to follow.

William Merritt Chase. *The Captain*. 1880. Oil on panel. 9⅞ x 5⅞". Private collection, Columbus, Ohio

William Merritt Chase. *A Subtle Device*. 1880. Oil on canvas. 11¾ x 19". Baker/Pisano Collection

Arthur Quartley. *The Sea Serpent as Seen by the Marine*. 1880. Charcoal and gouache on paper. 11¾ x 18". Private collection

Those who showed up for the 1880 excursion included Laffan, Weir, Smith, Quartley, Gifford, Dielman, Shinn, Sarony, Chase, Twachtman, O'Donovan, Reinhart, Knauth, Kobbe, and Charles Green Bush, a well-known illustrator and newly elected member of the club. The list of supplies was abundant, ranging from "a refrigerator nearly as big as a parlor in a French flat" to "two coops of chickens." Barely enough room remained for the passengers, who fortunately arrived in "light marching order."[91] The journey did not begin well; it was an unbearably hot day as O'Donovan guided the captain of the ship to the selected site. Since there was no dock, the travelers were forced to board small boats to reach the shore. O'Donovan, Dielman, and Knauth made the first trip to shore without incident. Chase, Laffan, and Shinn made up the second contingent, but before reaching land were confronted with an enormous wave that set them reeling into the sea. When they finally reached shore they were "battered, punched, buffeted, and banged to pieces."[92] Next came the unloading of the endless provisions and the setting up of quarters, which reportedly took six hours.

The first night the artists were said to have suffered from hallucinations, and the following morning, when they could not find any inspirational material, they relied on their purported nightmares to create fantastic visions of sea serpents: "one to a dozen designs of gigantic snakes, lashing the ocean with interminable coils, wrapping ships in their folds, and threatening the firmaments with their towering crests."[93] Quartley's *The Sea Serpent as Seen by the Marine* provided the reader with some indication of this fantastic creature as it might have appeared in a Grimm fairy tale; while Chase's version, *The Sea Serpent as Seen by 'Briarius'* (location unknown), is clearly derived from Elihu Vedder's painting *The Lair of the Sea Serpent*, 1864 (Museum of Fine Arts, Boston). Later that day, the Tilers were confronted by a real demon: the dreaded mosquito. "It was a dispensation like one of the plagues of Egypt," complained one of the artists.[94] Their troubles were relieved the next day when Baird, who had been wired in New York to bring mosquito netting, joined the group. By the fourth day, the inventive Chase used the netting to construct a makeshift outdoor studio in which he could

Edwin Austin Abbey. *Alfred Parsons*. 1881.
Pen and ink on paper. 11½ x 9"(sight).
Collection Graham D. Williford

paint unmolested by the pests. Chase's ingenious solution is depicted in his painting *A Subtle Device*, in effect, a self-portrait as a plein-air painter. In the background of Chase's composition are seen *The Two Sisters* and another Tiler lugging his heavy painting equipment in search of a suitable subject. At the end of the day the others returned with numerous sketches, but, unlike Chase's painting they were "fragmentary and incomplete."[95] That evening, frustrated by the forces of nature and the lack of artistic inspiration, Smith declared that he had had enough. The next morning Laffan agreed, claiming, "Nature is opposed to this business."[96] Quartley suggested the group give up their unsatisfactory quarters and move on to Port Jefferson, "a 'tiley' town by the sea, not far away — a place of peace and cheapness."[97] And, although the article continues as if this were an extension of the same trip, there is enough contradictory evidence to suggest that the story then leaps to yet another jaunt by the Tile Club to Long Island that happened more than a year later, in the fall of 1881.

Apparently, the group had not gathered enough illustrations or stories based on their aborted trip in the summer of 1880 to justify an article, which was tabled until additional material could be assembled. When plans were made for another summer trip to Long Island the following year (1881), there were some complications. Twachtman, who had married that spring, planned to travel to Europe with his new bride. Chase, who had been putting off travel abroad, was bound and determined to see the first work he had had accepted to the Paris Salon. Others may have had conflicts as well. To add to this, the group knew that Abbey, who had hoped to join them on Long Island, would not return to the United States until that fall. He also wanted his friend, the English artist Alfred Parsons, who was accompanying him, to take part in the excursion. Abbey had written enthusiastically to Parsons the previous year about his Tile Club experience on Long Island in 1878: "I never seemed to work so easily and surely as I did when I was with the boys on Long Island."[98] Meanwhile,

Edwin Austin Abbey. *At the Doorway.* 1879. Pen and ink on paper. 10⅞ x 6⅜". Private collection

This drawing was given by Abbey as a wedding gift to Lily Merrill on the occasion of her marriage to Francis D. Millet, March 1879. The wedding took place in Paris with Augustus Saint-Gaudens and Samuel L. Clemens (Mark Twain) as attendants.

another friend of Abbey's, Frank (Francis D.) Millet, had returned to New York and he, too, was interested in joining the contingent. Thus the trip was postponed until the fall of 1881.

Abbey and Parsons arrived in New York October 7, 1881, and shortly afterward, along with Charles Truslow (a young lawyer who was Abbey's cousin) rented 58½ West Tenth Street, a small house that would later serve as headquarters for the club.[99] In honor of their visit the Tile Club hosted a dinner with Smith (nicknamed "Owl") at the head of the table and Sarony ("Hawk") at the foot.[100] As whimsically reported, "Other ornithological and mythical bipeds [referring to the Tilers' sobriquets] surrounded the table and kept the 'guests' of the evening from flight."[101] It was likely at this time that Millet was made a member of the club, and Parsons and Truslow were asked to join as honorary members. Also, during one of Abbey's visits — perhaps this one — he arranged to have George H. Boughton made an honorary member. Boughton, an expatriate painter, was living in London and never attended a single meeting.

J. Alden Weir. *Port Jefferson.* 1881. Pencil and watercolor on paper. 6¾ x 9¾". Portland Art Museum, Portland, Oregon. Gift of Mr. and Mrs. William Ladd

F. Hopkinson Smith. *Home of the Artist William Sidney Mount.* 1881. Charcoal on paper. 12 x 17". Image taken from "The Tile Club Ashore," *The Century Magazine*, February 1882, Vol. XXIII, no. 4, p. 498

On October 26, 1881, the Tile Club finally made the journey to Long Island – destination: Port Jefferson. Those who participated were Abbey, Parsons, Laffan, Quartley, Millet, Baird, Chase, Weir, Dielman, Sarony, and William Agnew Paton, a newcomer to the group who was a writer and publisher of the *New York World*.[102] The trip, which lasted one week, proved to be much more successful than the one the previous summer. "The Tile Club Ashore," in *The Century Magazine* (February 1882), provided a composite account of the Tilers' two trips to Long Island as if it had taken place in the course of one excursion. A detailed description of Port Jefferson is supplied by Laffan as if it were promotional material for the Long Island Railroad, by which the group surely traveled: "There is a very old town, a sea-port, . . . surrounded by high hills and owning a deep land-locked harbor. It is not over fifty miles from New York, and is accessible by railroad which runs to the top of a hill a mile distant. . . . It is . . . rich in historical

interest . . . its people are . . . as sincere as if it had never known a summer boarder, and New York were a thousand miles away."[103] Indeed, it was also a "place of peace and cheapness," as Quartley had promised.[104] The Tilers immediately discovered an inn with rooms at an astonishingly low rate. Furthermore, it had both a piano and an organ for musical members. Unlike the previous summer, when the artists could find no artistic inspiration, this trip had landed them in an artist's paradise. Everything in the historic village related to either the making or dismantling of ships; even the local fences were crafted from the wreckage of old "ship-joinery."[105] These were "happy days of extemporized clam-bakes on the pebbly beach, of long swims in the clear blue waters of the harbor, of excursions through the hills and valleys of the Sound, of sketch books filled to overflowing. . . ."[106] Before leaving, the group paid homage to the area's most celebrated artist, William Sidney Mount (1807–68), by visiting his

F. Hopkinson Smith. *Elihu Vedder*. Pencil on paper. 8¾ x 6¼". National Portrait Gallery, Washington, D.C.

homestead, "a charming old Long Island household, a place rich in memories, and hallowed by endearing associations."[107] To commemorate the visit, Smith did a drawing of the Mount house, which was used in the article.[108] Although the days were dreary and filled with rain, they were days "that weather could not spoil," which in the travelers' minds "ended too soon."[109]

The year 1882 proved to be a very active one for the Tile Club, although not in the production of tiles, which had virtually ceased. One of the few members working in the decorative arts was the newly inducted Elihu Vedder.[110] In February of 1881, he had won a Christmas card competition sponsored by Prang and Company, which led to a commission that summer to do special midseason cover designs for *The Century Magazine*, including *Midwinter/ Number/February/1882*. Among Vedder's other decorative ventures were several done in collaboration with the J. and J. G. Low Art Tile Works. One was a relief tile done

Elihu Vedder. *Midwinter/Number/February/ 1882*, cover for *Scribner's*. 1882. Sepia ink on paper. 5¾ x 6". Kennedy Galleries, New York

in 1882 portraying the popular actress Anne Russell as "Esmeralda" in celebration of her one hundred fiftieth performance at the Madison Square Theater in New York. This was, however, a production piece that did not involve hand painting. By January of 1882, Vedder was attending the club's Wednesday night meetings and special events on a regular basis, and his diary entries give some insight into the schedule for that year. On January 12, the club held a reception for the poet Thomas Bailey Aldrich; on February 2, Vedder addressed the club; and on April 1 he created *the* drawing of the evening.[111]

Meanwhile, the February issue of *The Century Magazine* with the "Tile Club Ashore" article came out. And on February 25, an exhibition of works by Tile Club members was held at the St. Botolph Club, a private club in Boston established "for the promotion of social intercourse among authors and artists and other gentlemen connected with or interested in literature and art."[112] The exhibition was probably arranged by Millet, who was a charter member of the St. Botolph Club and who served on its 1880 Committee on Art and Library.[113] Contributors to the Boston exhibition were Quartley, Weir, Smith, Sarony, Gifford, Reinhart, Millet, Dielman, Vedder, Chase, Abbey, and Parsons. Based on the checklist, there is no indication that any of the fifty-two works shown were tiles. The range of subjects was broad, from views of Port Jefferson done by Smith and Parsons during the trip to Long Island in 1881 to scenes of Italy by Vedder, England by Parsons, Maryland by Dielman, and Germany by Chase. Also included were a fair share of figure pieces and portraits, including a portrait sketch by Chase of fellow Tiler Laffan. Underscoring the casual nature of the show, as well as the informal stylistic tendencies of the group, many of the paintings were described as "studies" or "sketches."[114]

In April of 1882, *The Century Magazine* published an article by Millet entitled "Some American Tiles."[115] This was a serious treatment of the development of tile manufacturing in the United States, in which he mainly discussed the work of John Gardner Low and the J. and J. G. Low Art Tile Works. Millet began by writing that the making of art tiles in America had begun so recently that most people knew nothing about it. He attributed this late entry into the field to the fact that the English had been producing such high-quality products that it discouraged Americans from trying to compete. However, he credited Low for being innovative in producing a new form of relief tile that had already won him a gold medal at the Crewe, England, exhibition of September 1880. Interestingly, Millet made no mention of the efforts of his own Tile Club, considered outside the mainstream of tile making. Also, it should be noted that there is no evidence that Millet, a relatively late inductee to the club, had ever painted any tiles himself.

When Abbey and Parsons returned to England in May of 1882, their small building at 58½ West Tenth Street became the official Tile Club headquarters for the next five years, although the group also continued to meet in each other's studios. Because of the cosmopolitan nature of the Tile Club and its transatlantic network of members, the clubhouse became, as described by Laffan, "a convenient neighboring planet . . . from which various points of the globe were precisely equidistant."[116] By this point Reinhart had settled in France; Abbey, Parsons, and Boughton were in England, where Millet would soon be as well; and the following year Vedder would return to his villa in Italy. All kept in close touch, and when club members traveled abroad they were warmly received by their brethren.

The clubhouse at 58½ couldn't have been better suited for the group. Its obscure location enhanced the club's carefully cultivated image of being exclusive and elusive. As Strahan (Earl Shinn) slyly informed the masses, "It is an undiscoverable place, burrowing out of sight, in harmony with the singular and notorious modesty of those who established it. There is no use, for those who have not received the password, in trying to find it."[117] He then tantalized his readers by luring them to the very doorstep with intriguing clues: "Find, if you can, the most inconspicuous of these entrances [on West Tenth Street], the kind of entrance which has two or three different numbers marked on it, and, if possible, some number 'and a half.'"[118] The house itself (still standing) is a small two-story structure built in 1835–36 and situated directly behind another period house (no. 58) built by the same family. To enter 58½, one had to proceed through a dark tunnel beneath the house fronting on the street.[119]

Beginning early in 1882, the Tilers were busy working on another joint venture, this time with *Harper's*. Tile Club artists were asked to contribute illustrations to accompany stories written by contemporary writers for a special Christmas edition of the magazine. Having submitted all the artwork by March, and with no organized summer sketching trip in the offing, the Tilers were free to "scatter themselves over Europe in search of rest and recreation, and to await in serene confidence the golden harvest of their reward" – referring to the *Harper's Christmas*.[120] Just prior to the release of this special issue, *Harper's Weekly* (November 25, 1882) published an article, "The Tile Club Abroad," a humorous account of members who had met in Paris that summer to attend the Paris Salon and see the sights. A series of cartoons by Reinhart (who was living in Paris) accompanying the article documents the antics of the travelers, although this was by no means an "official" Tile Club trip. Captions for the cartoon illustrations included "thrilling incidents on the voyage . . . meeting with exiled members of the club [including an image of Boughton done as if it were in tiles] . . . sightseeing . . . and breaking up."[121] The author (unidentified), criticizing Americans who viewed such recreation as a "frivolous waste of time," declared that the travelers returned not only refreshed, but "rich with the artistic spoils of many lands."[122]

Alfred Parsons. *River and Towing Path*. 1883. Oil on canvas. 24¼ x 60½". Philadelphia Museum of Art. John G. Johnson Collection

F. Hopkinson Smith. *The Hague.* 1882. Pencil,
watercolor, and gouache on paper. 12 x 23".
Courtesy Vance Jordon Gallery, New York

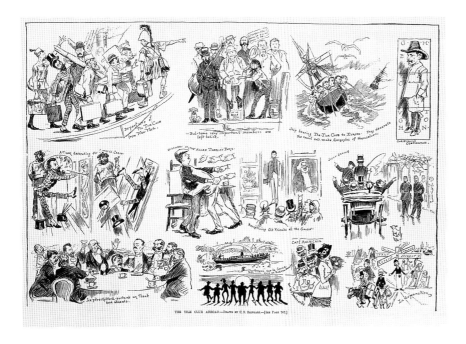

Charles S. Reinhart. Illustrations for
"The Tile Club Abroad" in *Harper's Weekly*,
November 25, 1882, Vol. XXVI, no. 1353,
p. 748

*The figure wearing the plaid suit is William Merritt
Chase, and it is his portrait, painted by J. Carroll
Beckwith, and his painting, Peter Cooper, on view
at the Paris Salon in the center right cartoon. The
"Exiled Tiler in Paris" (center left cartoon) is Charles
S. Reinhart, and the figure (upper right) is George H.
Boughton. The figures at the center rear of the table
(lower left) are Chase, R. Swain Gifford (with glass
raised), Edwin Austin Abbey, and Reinhart.*

When club members returned that fall they resumed their weekly meetings and parties. Among the special guests entertained earlier that spring were the actor Edwin Booth (May 3) and the writer Joel Chandler Harris. On December 9 they gathered at Smith's studio; on December 18 a party was held at Millet's studio for Oscar Wilde (in the United States for a lecture tour explaining the Aesthetic movement, "Lectures on the Decorative Arts"); and on December 19 a party was held at Gifford's place.[123] Surely at one of these events, the Tilers celebrated the release of the much anticipated *Harper's Christmas*, published both in America and England with amazing success.[124] This deluxe publication, printed on special paper, was graced with a beautiful cover design, *Luna*, by Vedder surrounded by a decorative border in mistletoe by Parsons. The issue included stories written by close friends of the Tilers (Mark Twain and Thomas Bailey Aldrich) and large drawings by club members, such as Chase's *The Burgomaster* and Vedder's *Samson*, which were

William Merritt Chase. *The Burgomaster*. 1882. Charcoal on paper. 28 x 18". Private collection, New York

Elihu Vedder. *Luna* (Study for *Harper's New Monthly Magazine*, Christmas Issue). 1882 (Border by Alfred Parsons). Pastel and watercolor on paper. 11¼ x 10⅛". Collection Graham D. Williford

particularly popular with the public. In fact, Vedder, in writing to his wife, reported that people were actually "cutting them out and framing them."[125]

The previous year the Tile Club had garnered international renown when an article appeared in the French publication *L'Art* (September 1881). The account focused on the publicity the group managed to generate for itself: "This unique organization peaked curiosity. From the outset, the Tile Club was in vogue. The stories which circulated, and illustrated journals which published exotic article after article, led the public to come to know the remarkable talent and appealing nature of the group."[126] So widely publicized were the club's activities that they caught the attention of Vincent van Gogh, who had seen both the *Harper's Weekly* article and the special *Harper's Christmas* issue. He wrote to his brother Theo in 1883: "At present there is a draftsmen's club in New York called the 'Tile Club' or the 'Tile Painters.'"[127] Expressing his particular admiration for Abbey, van Gogh specifically mentioned that he had a "little figure of a woman in the snow by him," perhaps the reproduction of *Winter* that appeared in *Harper's Christmas*.[128] In summary, van Gogh told his brother: "I write about it because I believe you will agree with me that not all Americans are bad. That, on the contrary, there are extremes there like everywhere else, and beside a lot of braggarts and daubers of the most detestable and impossible kind, there are characters who give the effect of a lily or a snowdrop between the thorns."[129] Clearly, it was through their widely appealing illustrations, rather than their tiles, that the Tile Club reached a broad public and gained invaluable recognition for its members.

The Tile Club was relatively inactive as an organization in 1883. Two early meetings were noted by Vedder, both dinners: one on January 27, the second organized by Smith and held on April 6 as a farewell party for Vedder, who was returning to Italy.[130] That summer Laffan traveled abroad, visiting Vedder in Italy and later spending two

Edwin Austin Abbey. *Winter*. 1882. Gouache on paper. 44 x 28". University of Cincinnati, Fine Arts Collection, Cincinnati. Gift of Engineering Class, 1923

days with Abbey, Parsons, and Boughton in Stratford, England, before returning home. A letter written by Millet to Vedder that fall reported that the club had begun to "peter out" after Vedder's departure from New York. The only real news was that Stanford White was made a Tiler (perhaps in place of Vedder).[131]

In the meantime, several of the club's more active members were busy with other ventures. Smith had taken on the awesome job as salaried director of the Pedestal Fund Art Loan Exhibition, which opened with a speech by him on December 3, 1883. This historic event was organized to raise funds to construct a pedestal for the Statue of Liberty presented by the French government to the American people on the anniversary of the country's independence. Other Tilers active in the organization of this show included Dielman, Millet, Augustus Saint-Gaudens (who became the club's second sculptor member around this time), and Chase, who served on a total of five committees, and was chairman of the Committee on Admission of Objects.[132] Chase also served as juror for the Munich Crystal Palace Exhibition of 1883, and was helping to plan the inaugural exhibition of the Society of Painters in Pastel (postponed until 1884). Now, several years after the production of tiles by the Tile Club had all but ceased, its crucial function as a fraternity and forum for struggling artists was diminishing as well.

One major accomplishment of the Tilers toward the end of 1883 was the remodeling of their clubroom at 58 ½ West Tenth Street. On January 3, 1884, Laffan wrote to Vedder that the club was not the same as it used to be.[133] Although the usual dinners and arguments were mentioned, nothing was said of regular Wednesday night meetings. A letter from Millet to Vedder provided further detail of the newly designed space created for them (two rooms had been renovated into one large L-shaped room) by their most recent inductee, the celebrated architect, Stanford White: "There is a light dado of red wood. Gorgeous Stanford White redwood mantlepieces and the

George H. Boughton. *A Daughter of a Knickerbocker*. 1880. Oil on panel. 14 x 8½".
Wadsworth Atheneum, Hartford

walls are all paneled off so as to admit canvases which are to be painted over by the members."[134] Suggesting the apathy of the Tilers by this point, Millet noted that not one of the vacant spaces left for the installation of paintings in the club's room had been filled, and although he, Quartley, and Gifford faithfully showed up for meetings, Weir turned up only "sometimes," Dielman "seldom," and Chase "rarely."[135] "There are too few of us who think it is a good thing to gather in the name of sociability," Millet summarized.[136] Rather than allow their newly furbished quarters to go to waste, they made them available to the Author's Club free of charge in hopes of establishing a little "fellow feeling between the two professions."[137]

A special event on February 20, 1884, brought many of the Tilers together for yet another excursion, this one probably an overnight trip. The occasion was a reception

Augustus Saint-Gaudens. *William Gedney Bunce*. 1877. Bronze. 7 x 5½". Collection Wadsworth Atheneum, Hartford

dedicating a new art gallery added to the home of the prominent Baltimore collector William T. Walters (1820–94). Among the Tilers who attended were Chase, Quartley, Laffan, Millet, Weir, Gifford, Sarony, and the honorary members Baird, Lewenberg, and Truslow. As noted in the local press, the painting that most impressed the Tilers was Théodore Rousseau's *Effet de Givre (The Hoarfrost)*, 1845. Done directly from nature as a finished painting rather than a sketch, this work was considered an important achievement in the development of plein-air painting. And it is significant that the Tilers, many of whom were experimenting with outdoor painting themselves, would have responded so noticeably to it.[138] Another diversion for several Tilers was political; Chase, Millet, and others were lobbying in Washington D.C. for the abolition of the unfair tariff recently imposed on the importation of foreign art. Additional personal matters distracted Tile Club members in 1884. Stanford White got married, and he and his wife traveled to Europe, visiting Vedder while in Italy; Chase spent the summer in Holland; Weir became a father; Quartley established a studio in London; and Millet moved with his family to Broadway, England. A new member was, however, added to the club, William Gedney Bunce, and an article, "Glimpses of the Tile Club," was released in *Art Amateur* (October 1884), with illustrations by Vedder, Abbey, Sarony, and Quartley, assuring the public the club was indeed still active.[139]

Little is known about the Tile Club's activities as a group in 1885, except that Laffan wrote Vedder's wife that they were doing "well, and had adopted a new drink, 'mint juleps.'" Laffan had meanwhile left *Harper's* to become publisher of the *Sun*; and several members, in addition to Weir, had, "with total disregard for income, become fathers of families."[140] Meanwhile, Millet was enjoying his home in Broadway hosting his old companions Abbey and Parsons and their new artist friend John Singer Sargent, made famous by his portrait, *Madam X*, at the Paris Salon of the previous year. Chase spent most of the summer in

William Gedney Bunce. *Venice, Sunrise*. Oil
on canvas. 23¾ x 36¾". Corcoran Gallery of
Art, Washington, D.C.

George W. Maynard. *Self-Portrait*. 1888. Oil
on canvas. 9 x 7". The Century Association,
New York

nearby London with yet another American expatriate
painter, James McNeill Whistler, where they were painting each other's portraits, to be exhibited together that
fall when Whistler returned home to the United States to
give a lecture tour. In fact, the Tile Club was gearing up
for a banquet to honor Whistler's return and serve as a
"send off" for his lecture tour, but the trip never materi-
alized. By the following year, Chase, tired of waiting for
Whistler to complete his portrait, which never was finished, and presumably was destroyed, exhibited *Portrait of
James Abbott McNeill Whistler* (Metropolitan Museum of
Art) without its companion piece (Whistler's portrait of
Chase).[141] The critics had a field day, mistakenly assuming
Chase's painting was a caricature of the notorious dandy
of Cheyne Walk. Whistler never spoke to Chase again!

In the spring of 1886, Abbey returned briefly to New
York and regaled Tilers, at a dinner held in his honor,
with stories about his new friend Sargent. It was about
this time that Shinn suggested that the club have an "At
Home" for the public. Laffan complained that there
was insufficient room in their small quarters. "There is
another kind of publicity which does not encroach on
anyone's room," Shinn countered in true Tiler fashion.[142]
"We'll just tease the outsiders by inviting the whole public to come and visit us. But in a peculiar way. . . . In a
book!"[143] And the idea became *A Book of the Tile Club*, published in 1887, to which many members contributed
their efforts.

The deluxe volume, the Tile Club's magnum opus,
measuring 15 x 12 ½ inches with 105 pages, was designed by
White and enhanced by endpapers adorned with members' seals (based on their sobriquets) cleverly devised by
the artist George W. Maynard, who at some indeterminate
point became a member of the club. The introductory
text was written by Shinn, and humorous accounts, loosely
based on facts, were contributed by Smith. Throughout
the book were sprinkled vignette drawings by the popular
illustrator Arthur B. Frost, presumably a recent inductee.

George W. Maynard. *Mermaids*. c. 1889. Oil on canvas. 18 ⅛ x 24 ⅛". Private collection

Arthur B. Frost. *Portrait of Emily L. Phillips.*
1881. Watercolor on paper. 14 x 9 ½". Private
collection, Montclair, New Jersey

William Merritt Chase. *A Summer Afternoon in Holland (Sunlight and Shadow)*. 1884. Oil on canvas. 65½ x 77¾". Joslyn Art Museum, Omaha, Nebraska

DECORATIVE AGE OR DECORATIVE CRAZE

—

Francis D. Millet. *A Handmaiden*. 1886. Oil
on canvas. 27 ⅛ x 16 ⅝". Leven Collection

Unfortunately none of these drawings has been located; however Frost's earlier work, such as his watercolor *Portrait of Emily L. Phillips*, shows an affinity to that of other Anglo-American Tilers such as Abbey and Boughton. The remaining illustrations ranged from informal sketches to full-page phototype plates of various members' major paintings. The subjects and styles of these accomplished works serve as testimony to the fact that the Tile Club, as a group, still did not represent any particular school of painting. Abbey and Millet, who had made England their adopted home, drew inspiration from its cultural heritage as seen in Abbey's *An Old Song*, a nostalgic costume piece based on earlier times, and Millet's *Handmaiden*, derived from the neo-classical revival made popular by English artists such as Lawrence Alma-Tadema. Similarly, Vedder, who had gained immeasurable celebrity from his illustrations for Edward FitzGerald's translation of the *Rubáiyát of Omar Khayyám* (1884), capitalized on this success with paintings such as *Pleiades*, indebted to the work of the English Pre-Raphaelite, Edward Burne-Jones. Weir's *Children Burying a Dead Bird*, on the other hand, reveals his continuing alignment with French painting, in this case the naturalism of Jules Bastien-Lepage. Maynard is represented by his *Portrait of a War Correspondent [Portrait of Frank Millet]*, an example of portraiture in the grand manner. Chase's contribution, *A Summer Afternoon in Holland*, leaning toward Impressionism, is by far the most advanced stylistically.

A Book of the Tile Club also served as an elegant coda to the club's existence. In 1887, Millet, in a letter to White, proposed Sargent for membership, but nothing seems to have come of it. Also, that year D. Maitland Armstrong bought 58 and 58 ½ West Tenth Street as a home for his family and the Tile Club was without a headquarters. The Tile Club, for all intents and purposes, had ceased to exist. Today, the hi-jinks, the sobriquets, the summer excursions, the debates and arguments, bespeak an era long past, one still remembered through the stories about, and especially the work of, members of the Tile Club.

Augustus Saint-Gaudens. *Francis D. Millet.*
1879. Bronze. 10½ x 6½". Collection Graham D. Williford

George W. Maynard. *Portrait of Francis D. Millet.*
1878. Oil on canvas. 59 ½ x 38 ¼". National
Portrait Gallery, Washington, D.C.

Augustus Saint-Gaudens. *William Merritt Chase.* 1888. Bronze relief. 21½ x 29½".
American Academy of Arts and Letters, New York

This work underscores the friendship between Saint-Gaudens and Chase, who most likely met as fellow Tile Club members. Although cast in 1888, Saint-Gaudens finished the sculpture in 1887, the final year of the Tile Club, and gave it to Chase in exchange for the painter's portrait of Saint-Gaudens (destroyed in a fire in Saint-Gaudens's studio in 1904).

Kenyon Cox. *Augustus Saint-Gaudens.* 1908 (Replica of original painted 1887 and destroyed by fire in 1904). Oil on canvas. 33½ x 47⅛". Metropolitan Museum of Art, New York

Although Cox was not a member of the Tile Club, he knew most of the artist members, and was a close friend of both Saint-Gaudens and Chase. His painting of Saint-Gaudens modeling the relief portrait of Chase was, most likely, given to Saint-Gaudens in exchange for a work by the sculptor, it being a common practice for friends to exchange works of art.

Stanford White. Title Page, *A Book of the
Tile Club*. 1887. Houghton Mifflin & Co.,
New York

Postscript

In the course of the decade (1877–87) in which the Tile Club was active, its focus quite naturally shifted. At the outset, its members chose as its ostensible purpose the decoration of hand-painted tiles. No serious effort was made, however, to promote or market their wares. In fact, the tiles they did produce were few, and remained outside the mainstream of development in this field. And, unlike their prototypes, the English craftsmen and women, members of the Tile Club never truly addressed the very special nature of tile design. Rather than treating their works in a decorative manner fully conceived in a patternlike way, they merely used the tile as another surface on which to paint. They continued to employ the usual devices of perspective and modulation of form to depict their subjects, whether landscape, portrait, or otherwise. In spite of their lack of adherence to the standard methods of this decorative form, they realized the special effects they could achieve in this medium; and those members who were most receptive and sophisticated used this knowledge to improve their own work as fine artists. The square format alone challenged new thought among future American Impressionist painters.[144]

Within a couple of years, however, the major proponents of tile painting left the group and the contingent of illustrators became stronger; the emphasis shifted to illustration, a focus that was sharpened by the success the group had with articles it produced for *Scribner's Monthly* and *The Century Magazine*. These popular periodicals provided a vehicle by which the artists could gain greater renown for themselves and for American artists in general. By maintaining, and even emphasizing, the exclusivity of the group – through limited membership, code names, and an elusive format – and continuing to produce entertaining stories accompanied by cleverly conceived and expertly executed illustrations, they generated invaluable publicity.

An unpremeditated benefit of the Tilers' summer sketching trips was their experience in plein-air painting, which proved to be invaluable to artists such as Chase, Weir, and Twachtman, who would ultimately be numbered among America's most noted Impressionist landscape painters. As teachers of outdoor painting, they would also have a profound effect on yet another generation of painters. In 1891, Chase established the first major school of plein-air painting in America, the Shinnecock Summer School of Art in Southampton, New York, on Long Island's South Fork. About the same time, Twachtman began teaching summer classes at Cos Cob, Connecticut, shortly afterward to be joined by Weir, who five years later directed his own outdoor classes at his home in Branchville, Connecticut.

In fact, the Tile Club provided an important social forum for its members, from the time they returned from their extensive studies abroad, sophisticated but penniless, to the time they emerged a decade later as successful artists who could resume their ties to the continent. In the closing paragraphs of *A Book of the Tile Club*, Earl Shinn aptly reveals the group's very special nature: "The ideas . . . discussed were produced unaffectedly from the Vatican, the thieves' quarter in London . . . . The streets of Naples, Vienna, and Algiers were about equally present in their minds; and they assembled around their friendly table in coats from Oxford and from Madrid, in shoes half worn on the sides of Vesuvius and in galleries of Gibraltar . . . All these comrades, challenging each other by names that were meaningless to the cold world."[145] Perhaps this statement, more than anything else, captures the essence of the Tile Club. Through their mutual experience, perseverance, and most important, their art, they managed in one decade to establish a new and more cosmopolitan identity for American art, as well as a greater appreciation and respect for a new breed of American artist.

Edward Burne Jones for Morris & Co.
Philomela and Dido from Chaucer's "Legend
of Goode Wimmen." 1873. Hand-painted
earthenware, each tile 5 x 5" (12.6 x 12.6 cm).
Private collection. Photo courtesy of
Haslam & Whiteway, Ltd., London

The tiles illustrated are from a set made for
Garboldisham Manor.

THE ART IN MANUFACTURE:

ENGLISH PAINTED TILES OF THE NINETEENTH CENTURY

By Mary Ann Apicella

The Arts and Crafts movement in Britain originated as a response to the Industrial Revolution, which radically changed the way in which goods were made during the late eighteenth and early nineteenth centuries. Objections to products overwroughtly imitative of European styles ultimately led to design reform, ceramic tiles both painted and printed, as we shall see, becoming a particularly favored medium within schemes to improve taste.[1] Reintroduced initially for the restoration of ecclesiastical projects, they ultimately became an art form closely associated with the British Aesthetic or Arts and Crafts movement, whose proponents sought the elevation of all media to the realm of fine art, all objects becoming worthy of artistic attention, including the lowly tile. The tile business, however, spurred on by Prince Albert, soon realized the immense industry potential of a material with enormous practical utility. By the end of the century, Britain was exporting vast quantities of its lusciously colored tiles to the four corners of the earth.

It was nineteenth-century Britain's great good fortune that a number of energetic personalities arose to devote their considerable talents to the elevation of artistic taste. The Roman Catholic architect and designer Augustus Welby Northmore Pugin (1812–52) deplored the spread of industrialization, and as an alternative model looked to the purposeful craft of the Middle Ages. Involved in the building or restoration of hundreds of churches and cathedrals, Pugin guided his friend Herbert Minton, the proprietor of a pottery in Stoke-on-Trent, to produce floor tiles appropriate to Pugin's ecclesiastical commissions.[2] It was another potter in Staffordshire, Samuel Wright of Shelton, however, who first patented the process for making encaustic floor tiles,[3] his firm eventually being absorbed by Herbert Minton's pottery in 1835.

Painted tiles were made in Britain earlier than the nineteenth century, but in 1843 pressing tiles from powdered clay was introduced, which allowed their rapid and uniform production. The practical applicability of a strong, nonporous, washable surface relatively impermeable to damp or dirt in coal-burning England was obvious. In addition to encaustic flooring tiles, Minton's was soon producing quantities of white tiles that could be painted.

At the Great Exhibition of 1851, the widespread admiration for Pugin's Gothic Court, which prominently featured Minton's majolica tiles, and the repetition of everything else brought to public attention the need for design reform. Convinced of the commercial advantages to British industry of good design, Prince Albert set up government schools throughout Britain to teach it, the free National Art Training School in South Kensington, later called the Royal College of Art, the most famous among them. Albert particularly encouraged the nascent tile industry by introducing tiling in a number of royal projects.

Albert's endeavors were augmented by the highly influential publications on ornamental design by Owen Jones (1809–74), an architect and "ornamentalist" who started his career working for a manufacturer of tiles and mosaics and continued to design tiles throughout his life. In 1856, he published a seminal work on design, *The Grammar of Ornament*, a lavish and brilliantly colored compendium of worldwide decorative patterns.[4] The startling flatness of the exotic, largely two-dimensional patterns Owen Jones reproduced was especially suited to the needs of a rising generation of trained "patternmakers." One of these was Christopher Dresser (1834–1904), a designer who worked for several potteries and, as the editor of the influential journal *Furniture Gazette*, published designs for tiles and articles about them.[5]

The 1867 Paris Exhibition was a showcase for the firm Morris, Marshall, Faulkner & Co., founded by William Morris (1834–96), a devoted pupil of the artist and art critic John Ruskin (1819–1900). In a lecture on "Modern Manufacture and Design" delivered in 1859, Ruskin encapsulated

Augustus Welby Northmore Pugin for Minton, Campbell & Co. *Encaustic Floor Tiles.* 1860–1865. Earthenware. Private collection. Photo courtesy Haslam & Whiteway, Ltd., London

Owen Jones. Plate 15. "Chinois Japonais."
The Grammar of Ornament. 1856. Chromo-
lithography on paper. Collection Haslam &
Whiteway, Ltd., London

William Morris. *Geoffrey Chaucer Reading.* 1864
Hand-painted earthenware, 6 x 6" (15.2 x
15.2 cm). Private collection. Photo courtesy
The Fine Art Society, London

his thoughts on decorative art, which had an enormous impact in both Britain and America. Ruskin's pronouncement of a formal theory by which easel artists could expand the scope of their artistic pursuits justified their endeavors in media other than painting and sculpture:

. . . [T]he only essential distinction between Decorative and other art is the being fitted for a fixed place; in that place, related, either in subordination or command, to the effects of other pieces of art. And all the greatest art which the world has produced is thus fitted for a place, and subordinated to a purpose. There is no existing higher order art but is decorative. . . . Get rid then at once of any idea of Decorative art being a degraded or a separate kind of art. Its nature or essence is simply its being fitted for a definite place: and in that place, forming part of a great and harmonious whole, in companionship with other art.[6]

William Morris applied this philosophy.[7] Morris designed all elements of the artistic interior, including tiles, as did the "artists of reputation" associated with his firm, Dante Gabriel Rossetti, Edward Burne-Jones, Ford Maddox Brown, Philip Webb, William de Morgan, and Albert Moore, who had been students together, Walter Crane, and others. Although early on most members of Morris's firm both designed and painted tiles, a division of labor between the designer and the painter later became typical in Britain as tile manufacturers, eager to associate their wares with good design, engaged artists to invent ranges of less costly and more widely salable printed tiles for them.

During the 1860s, however, Morris & Co. emphasized the hand-painted nature of its "art" tiles. Among the earliest were scenes from Chaucer's "Legend of Goode Wimmen," tales of ancient heroines who suffered out of devotion to their love; other pictorial themes followed. Morris & Co.'s painted tile production waned by 1871 because of its reliance on William de Morgan's ability to supply brilliant work in this field. William de Morgan (1839–1911), associated with Morris & Co. from 1863, was clearly the most talented ceramicist within the Morris circle, leaving it in 1869 to set up his own pottery. Initially

Walter Crane for the American Encaustic Tile Co. (1875–1935). *Tom Tucker.* c. 1880. Transfer printed and hand painted on earthenware, 6 x 6" (15.2 x 15.2 cm). Private collection. Photo courtesy Haslam & Whiteway, Ltd., London

Known primarily as a book illustrator, Walter Crane designed images that were especially suited to tiles. His images enjoyed enormous popularity in America.

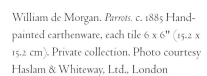

William de Morgan. *Galleons.* c. 1885 Hand-painted earthenware, each tile 6 x 6" (15.2 x 15.2 cm). Private collection. Photo courtesy The Fine Art Society, London

William de Morgan. *Parrots.* c. 1885 Hand-painted earthenware, each tile 6 x 6" (15.2 x 15.2 cm). Private collection. Photo courtesy Haslam & Whiteway, Ltd., London

trained as a painter, de Morgan was tantalized by the luster glazes on Persian pottery and eventually achieved iridescent effects in his own highly original stylized work.

Veering away from the ecclesiastical underpinnings of the Gothic revival, this younger generation of trained artist-designers freshened pedantic and archaeological modes of design into a search for beauty, utility, craft, and simplicity directed toward the middle classes. Morris, a socialist, had much to do with interjecting a moral component into this process, theorizing that many social evils resulted from disassociation from the product of one's work. Adherents of what was ultimately termed the Aesthetic or Arts and Crafts movement sought an environment filled with simple, hand-crafted, artful objects appropriate to their use.

In their quest, Morris and others embraced the art of Japan, viewing it as a country that had never lost an integrated art tradition, which they likened to their idealized vision of the Middle Ages. Oriental motifs – the fan, the chrysanthemum, sprays of almond or cherry blossoms –

asymmetrical compositions, and flat, nonillusionistic patterns appeared almost immediately in the work of artists and manufacturers. This also was the beginning of raging "Chinamania," the fascination with all forms of ceramics most usually manifested by the passionate collecting of Chinese porcelains, an obsession that swept up the Anglo-American painter James McNeill Whistler (1834–1903) and his circle, generating much musing on the nature of such artistry.[8]

Although the process of printing on tiles in color that it had perfected by 1855 ultimately became the lion's share of its product line, Minton's offered hand-painted tiles from its inception, and remained at the forefront of both industrial and artistic development in this medium throughout the century. In 1868, Minton's split into Minton, Hollins & Co., and Minton's China Works, the former producing mainly encaustic tiles and some picture series, and the latter wall tiles designed by some of the best known artists of the day.

Albert Moore for Minton, Hollins & Co.
January and February (opposite). 1875–90.
From a series of the months (above).
Hand-painted earthenware, each tile 6 x 6"
(15.2 x 15.2 cm). Collearn House Hotel,
Auchterarder, Scotland

The painter Albert Moore was a friend of Whistler's
and espoused similar Aesthetic sensibilities. Moore
designed tiles for William Morris early in his career,
as well as this subject, also done on white ground.

William Burges and Henry Stacy Marks. *Zodiac Tile Panel.* c. 1877. Hand-painted earthenware, 11 ½ x 38 ½" (29 x 97.3 cm). Private collection. Photo courtesy Blairman & Son, London

The medievalizing designer William Burges (1827–81) created a complicated cosmological program in tiles for the Summer Smoking Room at Cardiff Castle, Wales, that were likely painted by the American artist H. Walter Lonsdale.

Minton, Hollins & Co., "Ornamental Tile Mantelpiece." 1876. From Prof. Walter Smith, *Masterpieces of the Centennial Exhibition in Philadelphia, Vol. II.* (Philadelphia, 1876). Collection Haslam & Whiteway, Ltd., London

Oriental Themes. c. 1875. Hand-painted earthenware, each tile 6 x 6" (15.2 x 15.2 cm).
Thomas Goode, London

*A still-extant example of tiles used to decorate the
exterior of the exuberantly Arts and Crafts emporium
of Thomas Goode. Established in 1827, this firm
engaged Morris, Marshall, Faulkner & Co. to decorate
its interiors in the 1860s and sold tiles among its
offerings of china and pottery wares.*

William S. Coleman for Minton's Art
Pottery Studio. *Reclining Nude.* 1871–75. Hand-
painted earthenware, 18 x 24" (45.7 x 60.9
cm). Private collection. Photo courtesy The
Fine Art Society, London

*William S. Coleman favored a painterly style during
his direction of the short-lived Minton's Art Pottery
Studio, which burned down in 1875.*

Under the heading "Art Painted Tiles," a Minton,
Hollins & Co. catalogue asserted:

*The delicate and chaste painting on slabs of china is almost invariably
performed by ladies with a skill that compares favorably with similar
and much more pretentious work on canvas. . . . the painting of costly
tiles . . . [passes] . . . into the department of the artists, and these gentlemen place them upon their easels and . . . transform the plain squares
of clay into lovely pictures.*[9]

Minton's China Works, meanwhile, set up its own Art
Pottery Studio in South Kensington, which produced
high-quality painted pottery of all types, including tiles.
The company hired well known artists to design for them,
such as Walter Crane (1845–1915), whose illustrations for
children's books became popular designs for tiles, as well
as Christopher Dresser (1834–1904) and his associate
John Moyr Smith (1839–1912), described in the American
Harper's New Monthly Magazine as a "celebrated artist" who
created many popular designs for printed picture-tiles for
a number of potteries.[10]

Many other firms undertook large-scale painted tile commissions during this period, especially Doulton & Co., whose John Bennett (1840–1907) revitalized the Lambeth School of Art, from which Doulton's drew its talented painters, among them many women. Doulton's almost entirely relied upon its trained in-house artists, who became justly famous for their hand-painted specialities. Meanwhile, Doulton's executed spectacular projects such as the Indian apartments at the Cecil Hotel in London, which used thousands of hand-painted tiles.[11]

In 1865, plans to expand the South Kensington Museum by adding a lecture theater and three refreshment rooms beneath it were under way.[12] The progressive director, Sir Henry Cole, and the museum's own design team, chose to use ceramic tiles to decorate two out of three of these still-extant rooms. The East Dining Room, called the Grill Room, is entirely covered with Minton's tiles painted by the female students attending the National Art Train-

ing School's porcelain class between 1867 and 1869, which merged into Minton's Art Pottery Studio, originally organized for this project.

Divided into two levels, the lower portion consists of blue and white painted tiles arranged in alternating tiers of stylized fruit or flowers and painterly landscapes or seascapes, with a tier, just above the top, of larger tiles depicting females taken from myths. From the dado level to the ceiling are multicolored painted scenes evoking the four seasons on the west wall and the months of the year on the other three – all large figural studies executed on six-inch tiles.

The rich use of painted tiles in this most artistic and accessible of London public interiors was enthusiastically imitated in hotels, pubs, banks, hospitals, stores, public baths, private homes, and train stations. Because of their immense commercial use, tiles, both painted and printed, accounted for the most widespread dissemination of the imagery of the Arts and Crafts movement.

John Moyr Smith for W. B. Simpson & Sons. *The Months of the Year.* c. 1880. Hand-painted earthenware, each tile 6 x 6" (15.2 x 15.2 cm). Private collection. Photo courtesy Haslam & Whiteway, Ltd., London

Moyr Smith was described in the American Harper's Monthly Magazine *in June 1876 as a "celebrated artist," who created many popular designs for printed picture-tiles. W. B. Simpson & Sons, which began to describe itself as "art tile painters" around 1871, showed a painted version of this theme at the International Exhibition in Paris in 1878.*

Sir Edward Poynter, R. A. *The Grill Room.*
1867–68. Victoria and Albert Museum,
London. Courtesy the Trustees of the
Victoria and Albert Museum, London

*The tiles in this room were produced by Minton
Campbell & Co. before the firm divided.*

Sir Edward Poynter, R. A. *Landscape.* 1867–68.
Hand-painted earthenware, 12 x 12" (30.5 x
30.5 cm). Private collection. Photo courtesy
Haslam & Whiteway, London

*Blue and white tiles such as this appear on the art
market, which suggests that extras were produced.
The British Museum has an image of "Proserpine"
belonging to this project.*

The English display of tiles at the 1876 Centennial Exhibition in Philadelphia wowed the American public. The chef d'oeuvre of the Minton, Hollins & Co. exhibit was an ornamental tile mantelpiece decorated with "brilliantly plumaged birds."[13] Above this, a large tile picture of a young mother with her children was painted in sepia monochrome. Other Minton's painted panels of birds, flowers, and butterflies on a chocolate ground struck a contemporary observer as purely Oriental in design.[14] Doulton & Co. displayed a large tile picture of the departure of the Pilgrim fathers for America painted by their Mrs. Sparkes upon two hundred and fifty-two tiles, as well as story tile panels for mirrors and fireplaces.[15] The dazzling display of English ceramics unequivocally brought to American shores the role of tiles in revitalizing design, a point not lost on the reviewers of the exhibition:

Perhaps no better illustration of the improvement in the art of decorative design in England in the last quarter of a century can be found than in the study of the tiles made during that period.[16]

The response of the American public was enthusiastic – nearly fifty tile companies were established in America following the exhibition, numerous British ceramicists either emigrated to the United States or were hired by American firms, an explosion of books and articles on china painting appeared, associations to promote this activity proliferated, and the Tile Club was formed in 1877.

American artists had been traveling to Europe for art education since the 1830s, and several members of the Tile Club did so as well, Edwin Austin Abbey (1852–1911), George H. Boughton (1834–1905), and Frank Millet (1846–1912) being so culturally allied with England that they eventually expatriated. Aware of design trends there, American artists must nevertheless have been shocked and excited to encounter the innovative results of English design reform in a concentrated and comparative way at the Philadelphia show. Frank Millet worked as a newspa-

per and magazine correspondent at the exhibition and was no doubt aware of the presence of Christopher Dresser, who gave a series of lectures at the Pennsylvania Museum and School of Industrial Art before traveling to Japan at the behest of Tiffany & Co. of New York. Particularly interested in tiles, Millet wrote about them, and Abbey and Boughton were correspondents and illustrators for such American magazines as *Harper's Weekly* and *Scribner's Monthly,* which published decorating ideas encouraging the use of tiles.[17]

Also on American shores was the Scotsman Daniel Cottier (1838–91), aligned with the Morris circle and friend of John Moyr Smith. The embodiment of English reformist ideas, Cottier executed a number of projects from New York to Newport, and in 1879 undertook a smaller project, the manufacture of a picture frame designed by Tile Club member Stanford White and painted by an American artist Cottier particularly liked, Albert Pinkham Ryder.[18] Cottier also painted tiles, his most notable known, extant commission in the United States being those for the John Bond Trevor Mansion, now the Hudson River Museum in Yonkers, New York.

Cottier's wasn't the only enterprise painting tiles in New York during this period. At least three firms advertised themselves as professional pottery decorators during the 1870s,[19] and John Bennett, the director of the famed Doulton faience or earthenware department emigrated to New York in 1878 to teach pottery decoration at the newly established New York Society of Decorative Art. Renowned for the stylized asymmetrical natural forms and intense colors of his "Bennett ware," he left shortly to open his own pottery and was replaced at the Society by another talented ceramicist and former painter, Charles Volkmar, who exhorted his students to "treat the clay as one would a canvas."[20] These men imparted Aesthetic forms and ideas to those who aspired to artistic involve-

Daniel Cottier. *Guinevere*. Hand-painted
earthenware, Hudson River Museum,
Yonkers, New York

ment or crowded into art schools for perhaps more practical reasons:

*The recent mania for china . . . is being turned to account as a source
of income. There is hardly a village where women of artistic skill or
tastes are not trying to paint and bake china. The society on East 20th.
St. and others have established classes.*[21]

The Society of Decorative Art at 4 East Twentieth
Street and the Ladies Art Association at 28 East Eighteenth
Street were both founded to encourage the work of women
artists, regularly teaching classes in china painting, the
latter advertising that such classes were held twice a week.
By 1878, the free Women's Art School at the Cooper
Institute had 306 women students[22] and the *Crockery and
Glass Journal* ran a series of articles on pottery by J. C. L.
Sparkes (1833–1907), the headmaster of the National Art
Training School in South Kensington. In 1878, this jour-
nal also began publishing designs specifically for tiles.
Amateur pottery and glass painting flourished encouraged
by exhibitions for "Lady Amateurs and Artists" such as
those held by the Society of Decorative Arts, which met
with "abundant success."[23]

It was against this backdrop of extreme public engage-
ment with the artistry of ceramics that the Tile Club was
formed. In choosing to associate themselves with tiles, a
material inseparable from the intent and imagery of English
design reform, its members perhaps mimicked the ladies
of the china painting clubs, but nevertheless set themselves
in the forefront of the Aesthetic intentions of the era.

Charles Yardley Turner. *A Saturday Evening
at the Century Association*. 1894. Oil on canvas,
25⅞ x 35⅞". The Century Association,
New York

BOHEMIANS AND BUSINESSMEN:

AMERICAN ARTISTS' ORGANIZATIONS OF THE LATE NINETEENTH CENTURY

By Linda Henefield Skalet

A distinctive characteristic of American society in the decades following the Civil War was a proclivity to organize into special interest groups. These groups ran the gamut from baseball and yachting clubs, to political and social clubs, to professional associations like the Grange (1867), the American Library Association (1876), the American Bar Association (1878), the American Society of Chemical Engineers (1880), and the American Forestry Association (1882). American artists were no exception to this phenomenon, founding literally hundreds of organizations, the most important of which were located in New York.

The creation of late-nineteenth-century artists' organizations was part of a larger movement toward special interest promotion and professional self-definition in response to the increasing complexity of American society.[1] Earlier artists' organizations in America had grown out of the need for fellowship and a shared interest in the refinement of artistic skills. The Sketch Club had been formed in

New York in 1829 by members of the infant National Academy of Design (1826), including Academy instructors Samuel F. B. Morse, Charles C. Ingham, Thomas S. Cummings, and Asher B. Durand. The organization of the group followed the late-eighteenth-century tradition of English sketching clubs.[2] Artists and literary men met every other Friday night at the home of one of the members, who supplied pencils, paper, a subject for the evening's work, and modest refreshments. Members sketched or wrote poetry for an hour and socialized afterward.[3] Subjects for sketching ranged from the mysterious and evocative ("Deserted Village" or "The Abduction"), to the biblical ("Cain Slaying Abel"), to the literary (Lord Byron's "Darkness" or the Elfin Page from Sir Walter Scott's "Lay of the Last Minstrel"), and the evening's work became the property of the host.[4]

Though serious work was done at these meetings, it is clear from the minutes that there was much fun as well.

Samuel F. B. Morse. *Scene with the Elfin Page,*
from Scott's "Lay of the Last Minstrel." 1829.
Pencil on paper, 8 x 10". Yale University
Art Gallery

Brief entries record "Champagne! . . . . Sketching Slim."
(April 8, 1830), "Singing and lots of fun." (April 1, 1831),
"Champagne, singing and sketching." (April 8, 1831).[5] The
artists were high-spirited men in their twenties and thir-
ties; the club's form, youthful spirit, and Bohemian atmosphere were substantially repeated in the clubs formed by
similar groups of young artists in the 1870s and 1880s.

By 1847 the Sketch Club members were older and
wealthier; now they wanted a clubhouse with easy chairs,
a kitchen with a chef, and the capacity for a larger membership. Consequently, Asher B. Durand, John G. Chapman,
Charles C. Ingham, Francis W. Edmonds, Abraham M.
Cozzens, and Henry T. Tuckerman called a meeting that
resulted in the founding of a new club to "be composed
of authors, artists, and amateurs of letters and fine arts,
residents of the city of New York and vicinity. Its objects
shall be the cultivation of a taste for letters and the fine
arts, and social enjoyment."[6] The Century Association
was not primarily the domain of artists, but its broader
membership served the purposes of the artist members

by providing an opportunity to socialize with the wealthy
amateurs of New York — the lawyers, bankers, and businessmen who bought art. The club also assembled its own
collection of works by its artist-members, by either buying their paintings or sculptures or accepting them in lieu
of initiation fees. However, the most important advantage
to the artists was the regular exhibition of their work.

By the 1870s, the exhibition of recent work by artist-
members had become a feature of Century's monthly
meeting.[7] These shows provided an opportunity for artists
to test the response to their work before releasing it to
the public at large or submitting it to the Academy exhibitions. The current show was also discussed and criticized
by the membership. Century member Jervis McEntee's
diaries reveal the import of these discussions. He wrote on
February 7, 1885, with apparent anxiety, "I sent my picture
of the winter sunset to the Century and so much depends on
its success and I am so afraid that I will feel disappointed."[8]

The Century Club set an important example for other
New York clubs. By 1873, the Lotos Club had a monthly
exhibition schedule and by the early 1880s the Union
League was also hanging monthly shows. In the 1890s, the

Thomas Cole. *Scene with the Elfin Page,* from
Scott's "Lay of the Last Minstrel." 1829.
Pencil on paper, 8 x 10". Yale University Art
Gallery

Photograph of the exterior of the Century Club, 109 East Fifteenth Street. c. 1870

Photograph of the art gallery of the Century Club's Fifteenth Street clubhouse. c. 1870

Paintings displayed are probably for members to view at a regular monthly meeting.

Alpha Delta Phi Club, Colonial Club, Hamilton Club, Heights Club, Lambs Club, Manhattan Club, and New York Athletic Club were all sponsoring art exhibitions.[9]

The Palette Club appeared in New York in 1869. It had "for its intention the bringing together of artists, the reading of papers on artistic and philosophical subjects and the exhibition of art products by the members."[10] Like Century, Palette included more amateurs than artists in its membership, and they were expected to buy the artists' work when it was exhibited. In his 1873 book, *The Clubs of New York,* Francis Gerry Fairfield explains, "I think the founders of the Palette had dimly in mind, when they framed the first constitution, an idea of eliminating the middle-men."[11]

The Palette Club's projects addressed the most keenly felt needs of New York artists in the 1870s. In addition to providing opportunities for exhibition and sale, the club had an art school and a library of books on art. Artists made up one-quarter of the nearly five hundred members in 1873 and included successful older Academicians like William Page, James H. Beard, John W. Ehninger, William Hart, and Albert Bierstadt; younger members of the Academy like Winslow Homer and John Lafarge; very young artists like Will Low and Frank M. Gregory; and the ubiquitous Napoleon Sarony. What is surprising is that within just a decade the club had changed its orientation and, according to *Scribner's Monthly,* had "declined as a place of artistic resort and is now said to contain layman only."[12] Perhaps the businesslike relationship that the club set up between artists and amateurs did not foster real fellowship.

The Salmagundi Club began in 1871 as a group of young art students and their nonartist friends who met Saturday nights in the studio of Jonathan Scott Hartley at 596 Broadway to sketch and socialize. Following the model of the Sketch Club, they chose one subject for all to sketch: "Wind," "Hell," "A Frosty Morning," "Calm," "Something Fresh," "Extremes Meet," "Happy as a King," "Weirdness," "Silence," and "Conviviality."[13] Drawings were prepared on the proposed topic during the week, rather than at the meeting, and critiqued the following week. Meetings began with the exhibition and discussion of sketches and proceeded to eating, drinking, smoking, singing, storytelling, boxing, and fencing.

In a drawing done to illustrate "Young Artist's Life in New York," which appeared in *Scribner's Monthly,* Will Low portrays a typical Saturday night at Hartley's studio during the early years of the club.[14] Hartley, in the foreground cooking sausages, is raising his left arm to warn the boxers away from his stove. At the left, Hartley's younger brother John, one of the laymen in the group, is setting the makeshift table. Harry P. Share sits on a turntable smoking in the right foreground. Behind him are Milton J. Burns and Alfred Becks, a young English actor visiting for the evening. William H. Shelton is seated behind and to the right of the boxers. The group behind him peruses the evening's sketches, which are hung on a screen.[15] The atmosphere is young, masculine, and Bohemian, a characteristic that by 1880, when the drawing was published, had acquired considerable cachet.

Another illustration in the same article, drawn by Harry P. Share, shows an 1879 meeting of the club (now the Salmagundi Sketch Club). The membership looks older, more prosperous, and considerably more conventional. Hartley still occupies the central position, but he has traded his cooking apron for tie and tails. Boxing and fencing have given way to genteel conversation, but the week's drawings are still visible hanging on the walls to be critiqued.

In 1878 the club began its annual exhibitions of black and white drawings. This particular medium was suited to the Salmagundi artists, most of whom were actual or aspiring illustrators for the many weekly and monthly publications of the period such as *Harper's, Appleton's, Scribner's,* and *Frank Leslie's.* The Black and White Exhibitions, which included both members' and non-members' work, became popular annual events in New York, drawing

Will H. Low. *Boxing in Hartley's Studio.*
1879. Watercolor on paper, 17 x 22".
The Salmagundi Club, New York

appreciative crowds to the Academy and the American Art Association, where they were held, and eliciting consistently favorable reviews from the critics. About half of the exhibitions resulted in a profit for the club, but even those that did not profited the artists by bringing their work before the public. The shows continued until 1888, by which time advances in technology had made inexpensive reproductions of famous paintings available to the public, ruining the market for original drawings.

In view of the cessation of the Black and White Exhibitions and the waning interest in weekly sketching, the sixty-five members of the Salmagundi Sketch Club voted to drop the word "sketch" from their name and become a social club. They initiated a schedule of art exhibitions much like the Century Club's, but with three significant differences: most of the art shown at the Salmagundi Club was for sale at prices indicated in printed catalogues; exhibitions were not restricted to the work of club members; and the public was invited. According to one New York newspaper, "One of the best features of the Salmagundi exhibitions is the chance offered by them to furnish a place where those who buy American art can familiarize themselves with what is going on in the many studios without making special visits to the artists."[16] This club's membership, which was composed primarily of working artists, was keenly aware of the necessity of marketing their work and made every effort to make it available to the art-buying public.

In its new role as a social club, Salmagundi was committed to being "the art club of New York" and to holding on to its reputation for Bohemianism,[17] and reports in the New York daily press show that it succeeded. *The World, The Sun,* and *The Herald* all delighted in describing the club's artistic revelries and wild entertainments. As William H. Shelton explains in his history of the club, "The New York dailies were very attentive to the movements of the Salmagundi, partly because of its activity in art matters, and partly because the press seemed to regard

Howard Pyle. *Something Fresh.* 1878. Location unknown. Published 1918 in William H. Shelton's *The Salmagundi Club: A History.*

Charles S. Chapman. *The Salmagundi Clubhouse, 14 West Twelfth St.* 1898. Charcoal on paper, 30 x 21". The Salmagundi Club, New York

Charles S. Chapman. *The Art Gallery, 14 West Twelfth St.* 1898. Charcoal on paper, 21 x 30". The Salmagundi Club, New York

Napoleon Sarony. *Self-Portrait.* c. 1895.
Photograph. Collection Janet Lehr

the club as a sort of Bohemian morsel that it loved to turn over in its journalistic maw and upon which it never tired of regaling itself."[18]

The Tile Club, also known for its Bohemianism, attracted the admiring attention of the popular press almost immediately. *Scribner's Monthly* published three articles about the club in 1878, 1879, and 1880, each one longer and more lavishly illustrated than the last. A fourth appeared in *Scribner's* successor, *Century Magazine,* in 1882. Readers were introduced to the club's members and their work and invited to participate vicariously in their Bohemian adventures.

The lure of Bohemia was a favorite theme of the period's magazines. In 1879–80, *The Art Journal* presented a three-part series on "Studio Life in New York" in which the flamboyantly decorated studios of Tile Club members William Merritt Chase and R. Swain Gifford were featured. It described New York's Bohemia, the neighborhood around Washington Square: "This is the republic composed of the artist fraternity, and it presents many phases prolific in interest to those who love to wander from the high-road and seek in the lanes and byways of Bohemian or quasi-Bohemian life for scenes and suggestions which 'respectability with its thousand gigs' cannot furnish."[19]

The exciting and amusing aspects of Bohemia, without the sordidness or scandal of Henri Murger's Parisian original, are what the Tile Club and Salmagundi Club artists embodied. Potential patrons, who read with amusement and not a little envy the chronicles of their escapades, could also share in the freedom and adventure of their lives by visiting their studios and buying their work. Thus, without holding exhibitions, but merely by its extraordinary appeal to the public, the Tile Club succeeded in marketing its members' work. Flamboyant and unconventional, as artists ought to be, they were, nonetheless, entirely respectable, so much so that fifteen of the twenty-eight members gained entry into the most selective of New York clubs, the Century.

In 1881, another small artists' club arose out of New York's Bohemia. The Kit Kat Club was organized by Napoleon Sarony, Edward Moran, William H. Lippincott, Charles Yardley Turner, Thure de Thulstrup, and Graham Clarke. Nym Crinkle, aka A. C. Wheeler, wrote a lengthy article illustrated by club members for the *Quarterly Illustrator* in 1894. According to Wheeler, the organizers could not find the artistic fellowship they desired in the existing clubs of New York. They wanted "a meeting place that would be a rendezvous, without being a salon; a sitting-room and not a parlor. A club without a kitchen . . . artistic intercourse without hiring a butler or paying a cook. They didn't want to be Bouguereaus, but Bohemians."[20]

In 1881, Sarony, Turner, and de Thulstrup belonged to the Salmagundi Club, which it is hard to believe they would have found too formal and conventional. Salmagundi had no cook, butler, or even a regular meeting at the time. Sarony was a member of the Tile Club as well, also no haunt of an aspiring Bouguereau. Perhaps they wanted a younger group, which Kit Kat was, or one that excluded laymen from its membership, which Kit Kat did. However, it is more likely that they just wanted another club to belong to. Many Americans of the period typically held membership in numerous organizations at the same time. Sarony, who served as Kit Kat's first president and in whose studio the group met, belonged to the Palette, Salmagundi, Tile, Kit Kat, Arcadian, and Lotos clubs, and was a visible presence in each.

Kit Kat provided its members with live models to draw several nights a week, held Saturday night "smokers" to which the New York art community was invited to socialize and view members' work, organized summer sketching trips (as did the Tile Club), and held several sales of sketches each year and a large annual exhibition. It also took pains to preserve its Bohemian aura. By the mid-1890s, Bohemianism had become a national fad with the publication of William Dean Howells's *The Coast of Bohemia* in 1893, George Du Maurier's *Trilby* in 1894, and numerous magazine articles, including A. C. Wheeler's on the Kit Kat Club.[21] The adoption of a visible Bohemian lifestyle by American artists was good for business. Perhaps this explains, in part, the founding of the Kit Kat Club and its interest in maintaining the image that Wheeler created in print: "I really believe that to-day the Kit Kat is the only really Bohemian club we have — in the best sense of that word. . . . [I]t is the only place where you can escape from the conventionalities without tumbling over the improprieties."[22] What Wheeler alluded to was the same sort of genteel, nonthreatening Bohemianism that had made the Tile Club so popular fifteen years earlier.

James David Smillie, R. Swain Gifford, and Dr. Leroy Milton Yale. *First Etching of the New York Etching Club.* 1877. Etching, 2⅜ x 3½". Old Dartmouth Historical Society, New Bedford, Massachusetts

Organizations exclusive to professional artists in New York date back to the founding of the National Academy of Design in 1826. The Academy served the interests of the profession adequately until after the Civil War, but in the 1860s through the 1890s many new organizations were founded to address the needs of artists working in specific media or whose work was perceived to be in opposition to the prevailing style of the Academy.

The American Watercolor Society was founded in 1866. Samuel Colman, William Hart, William Craig, and Gilbert Burling, who served as the organization's first officers, called a meeting for "the formation of a society to promote the art of Water Color painting in America."[23] The public needed to be educated as to the true potential of the medium, which many Americans considered a technique for amateurs or for preliminary sketches for oil paintings. They also believed that watercolors were perishable because they were done on paper, and thus undesirable to buy. To address these prejudices an explanatory article about watercolor painting written by the officers appeared in the catalogue of the Society's second exhibition, and was subsequently reprinted as a pamphlet and widely distributed.

Apart from dispelling common myths about watercolor and reviving its reputation, the primary focus of the organization was the exhibition and sale of works in the medium. Its first annual exhibition was held at the National Academy of Design the winter of 1867–68 in conjunction with the Academy's Winter Exhibition. The Academy's prestige was an important factor in its success. For the next five years the Society continued to exhibit with the Academy, but in 1873 it asserted its independence. The entire Academy building was rented for the seventh annual show, which proved to be the largest and most successful exhibition to date.

The Watercolor Society's annual exhibitions enjoyed similar success for most of the next decade. More prestigious artists like J. A. M. Whistler, Thomas Eakins, Winslow Homer, Thomas Moran, and Eastman Johnson submitted their work, and American taste for watercolors grew. The Society's promotional efforts were, at least in part, responsible for both phenomena. The society's officers solicited artists for work to exhibit by mailing out hundreds of letters, which included practical marketing advice such as recommendations for framing.[24] In 1870, the Society instituted a third membership category, "honorary," to include the patrons who were critical to their financial success, and they made sure that their exhibitions were advertised in the daily newspapers. They also hung banners on the Academy's exterior, gave out free tickets to members of the Academy and to merchants willing to display their posters, and distributed thousands of circulars before and during the shows.

Both the Art Students League and the Society of American Artists grew out of the conflict between the older generation of American artists who controlled the Academy and the "new men" who had returned from their training in Munich and Paris in the 1870s. While the Art Students League concerned itself with the education of the younger generation, the Society of American Artists addressed the problems of exhibition and sale. The society was formed in 1877 by a group of young, mostly European-trained artists led by Augustus Saint-Gaudens, Walter Shirlaw, Wyatt Eaton, and Helena deKay Gilder. They were convinced that the Academy's policies were biased toward more conservative artists and that they had little chance of having their work seen in Academy exhibitions. Seeing no hope of resolving what was both a generational conflict and a battle of styles, they created a new organization. The society's first annual exhibition in March of 1878 demonstrated its commitment to representing the new movements of the day. One-third of the exhibition space was allotted to Americans studying in Paris, one-sixth to those in Munich, Rome, Florence, and other European cities, and the remaining half to Americans at home. The Society's annual exhibitions, which were held each spring for the following twenty-seven years, provided an important additional opportunity for American artists to show their work.

Though women were not accepted as members of the artists' clubs, they were included from the outset in the professional organizations. The American Watercolor Society, the Art Students League, the Society of American Artists, and the New York Etching Club all had women members. The Society of Decorative Arts was conceived in 1877 as a professional organization exclusively for women. Candace Wheeler, whose brainchild it was, recruited a group of wealthy New York women active in the fine arts to help establish an educational and commercial institution. She envisioned a place with rooms for the exhibition and sale of decorative arts; classrooms for instruction in embroidery, drawing, china painting, and pottery decoration; workrooms to execute commissions; an art and craft supply store; and a lending library on the decorative arts. Her goals were to provide employment for women and to restore the decorative arts, and ornamental needlework in particular, to the high place that they had once occupied among the arts.[25]

Wheeler's plans came to fruition in a remarkably short time owing to the generous support of the Society's subscribers and the proceeds from the two loan exhibitions it held at the National Academy of Design in the winter of 1877–78 ($7,940.20) and the fall of 1878 ($4,329.51).[26] In 1878, the first full year of the Society's existence, the salesroom reported $22,776.39 in sales. The workrooms had received and executed 1,074 orders, employing five or six women continually and another thirty-seven from time to time. Classes in art needlework had been attended by 198 students, china painting classes by 151 students, and private lessons given to another sixty-three.[27] Once established, the organization continued to flourish.

The American Watercolor Society provided the model for other organizations dedicated to the revival of media that had fallen into disrepute. The New York Etching

Club was formed to promote "painter-etching" and to teach artists its techniques. More than half of the seventeen artists who attended the club's first meeting in James D. Smillie's studio on May 2, 1877, knew nothing about the technical process of etching. Consequently, the highlight of the evening was the etching of a demonstration plate by Smillie, who ground the plate; R. Swain Gifford, who drew the design; and Dr. Leroy Milton Yale, an amateur who pulled the first proof.[28] Following this, the group, which included Charles Henry Miller, Edwin Austin Abbey, Frederick Dielman, Louis Comfort Tiffany, Henry Farrer, and Samuel Colman, met the second Monday of each month in order to refine their skills.

By 1879 they were ready to begin exhibiting their work, initiating a series of annual exhibitions that helped create an enormous popularity for etching during the 1880s. In 1882 the Society of Painters in Pastel began a campaign to revive that medium. Though its members proceeded with considerably less rigor in organizing and holding exhibitions, their efforts, nonetheless, contributed to the increasing popularity of pastel. Other special interest organizations founded included the Woman's Art Club of New York (1889), the National Sculpture Society (1893), the American Society of Mural Painters (1895), and Ten American Painters (1898).

A revealing picture of the situation of American artists in the late nineteenth century emerges in this chronicle of artists' organizations. They were both the makers and the marketers of their work, as the art dealers of the period were more interested in promoting European than American art. Artists found the clubs of New York, whose memberships included so many wealthy amateurs, to be useful in locating patrons. They also found that these potential patrons were attracted to the popular image of the artist as a "free spirit." As a result, they encouraged that romantic perception of themselves, while at the same time devising strategies to promote, exhibit, and sell their work. In short, they had to be both Bohemians and businessmen.

NOTES

Decorative Age or Decorative Craze

1. Thorstein Veblen, *The Theory of the Leisure Class*, 1899 (Reprint. New York: The Modern Library, 1931), p. 209. Although the term "conspicuous consumption" was coined by Veblen over a decade later, it is applicable to what was developing in American society at the time.

2. For a full discussion on this topic, see Doreen Bolger Burke, "Painters and Sculptors in a Decorative Age," *In Pursuit of Beauty: Americans and the Aesthetic Movement* (New York: The Metropolitan Museum of Art/Rizzoli, 1986), pp. 294–339.

3. Linda Henefield Skalet, "The Market for American Painting in New York: 1870–1915" (unpublished Ph.D. dissertation, John Hopkins University, 1980).

4. William Mackay Laffan, "The Tile Club at Work," *Scribner's Monthly*, XVII, No. 3 (January 1879), pp. 401–409.

5. For detailed biographical sketches on each artist member see: Constance Eleanore Koppelman, "Nature in Art and Culture: The Tile Club Artists/ 1870–1900" (unpublished Ph.D. dissertation, State University of New York at Stony Brook, 1985). This is the most comprehensive source on material relating to the Tile Club; however, with all secondary sources about this elusive group, facts must be carefully rechecked and confirmed. This is not meant to demean Ms. Koppelman's impressive research and extensive biographies, for which I am indebted.

6. F. Hopkinson Smith and Edward Strahan [Earl Shinn], *A Book of the Tile Club* (New York: Houghton Mifflin & Co., 1887) p. 5.

7. Laffan, p. 401.

8. Ibid.

9. Ibid.

10. Ibid., p. 402.

11. Ibid.

12. Letter from Edwin Austin Abbey to Will Low (1908) quoted in E. V. Lucas, *The Life and Works of Edwin Austin Abbey, R. A.* (New York: Scribner's, 1921), Vol. I, p. 47.

13. Laffan, p. 402.

14. Ibid.

15. Ibid.

16. Ibid.

17. Ibid., pp. 402–403.

18. Smith, p. 9.

19. As a means of deciphering these sobriquets see: William R. Shelton, "Autobiography," (Washington D. C.: Archives of American Art, c. 1920, Roll No. 800); and J. B. Millet, "The Tile Club," *J. Alden Weir: An Appreciation of His Life and Work*, The Phillips Publications, No. 1 (New York: E. P. Dutton & Co., 1922).

20. Primary sources have variously identified Paris's studio at "1" and "3" Union Square. Shelton (cited above), who claims he took over the studio from Paris, lists the address as "3" and provides a description.

21. Laffan, p. 403.

22. Smith, p. 5.

23. For technical background and English derivations see Althea Callen, *Women Artists of the Arts and Crafts Movement* (New York: Pantheon Books, 1979).

24. Smith, p. 5.

25. F. Hopkinson Smith, *The Fortunes of Oliver Horn* (New York: Scribner's Sons, 1902), p. 432. Smith provides an account loosely based on the Tile Club in Chapter XX, "The Stone Mugs," and Chapter XXI, "The Woman in Black." Interesting as these accounts are, none can be taken as pure fact.

26. Smith, p. 6.

27. Ibid.

28. Laffan, p. 407.

29. All technical details have been derived from two basic primary sources, as listed above: Laffan, and Smith and Strahan.

30. For numerous related works done at

Mountainville, New York, see: Gordon Hendricks, *The Life and Work of Winslow Homer* (New York: Harry N. Abrams, Inc., Publishers, 1979). This source also includes discussion on Homer's tile and tile fireplace surrounds.

31. See Burke, p. 338, who in footnotes 71–72 credits Lloyd and Edith Havens Goodrich for providing extensive information on Homer's tiles (correspondence, April 6, 1984).

32. Ibid.

33. Laffan, p. 409.

34. Ibid.

35. Ibid.

36. Ibid.

37. See: Ronald G. Pisano, *Long Island Landscape Painting: 1820–1920* (Boston: Little Brown & Co., 1985), p. 59, for illustration of *East Hampton Beach, Long Island*, 1874 (Collection of Mr. and Mrs. Paul Mellon).

38. Laffan, p. 409.

39. William Mackay Laffan and Edward Strahan [Earl Shinn], "The Tile Club at Play," *Scribner's Monthly*, XVII, No. 4 (February 1879), pp. 457–478.

40. Laffan, "The Tile Club at Work," p. 406.

41. Laffan and Strahan, p. 459.

42. Ibid., p. 461.

43. Ibid.

44. Ibid., p. 465.

45. Ibid.

46. Ibid.

47. Ibid., p. 471.

48. Ibid., p. 475.

49. Ibid., p. 477.

50. For an illustration of this work see Hendricks, p. 113, figure 169, *David Pharaoh, the Last of the Montauks, July 21,* 1874, watercolor with pencil, 11¾ x 10 (Private collection).

51. Ibid., p. 478.

52. William Mackay Laffan, *The New Long Island: A Handbook of Summer Travel,* (New York: Rogers & Sherwood Publishers, 1879). References to the Tile Club include: pp. 15–17; 30–35; 39–44.

53. William Mackay Laffan and Edward Strahan [Earl Shinn], "The Tile Club Afloat," *Scribner's Monthly*, XIX, No. 5 (March 1880), p. 642.

54. Ibid., pp. 641–671.

55. Ibid., p. 644.

56. Ibid.

57. Letter from R. Swain Gifford to his wife Fanny (June 29, 1879), provided by Richard C. Kugler, Director Emeritus, New Bedford Whaling Museum, New Bedford, MA. According to this letter, the group left New York on Friday evening, so by the time they neared Albany at the date of the letter, Thursday, June 29, they would have been traveling six days, which is consistent with the article which states they left on June 23rd; however, the article suggests a much shorter timespan from when they left New York until they reached Albany.

58. Ibid.

59. Ibid.

60. Laffan & Strahan, p. 647.

61. Ibid., p. 648.

62. Ibid., p. 649.

63. Ibid., pp. 649–650.

64. Ibid., p. 650.

65. Ibid.

66. Ibid.

67. Ibid., p. 656.

68. Ibid., p. 665.

69. Ibid., p. 667.

70. Ibid., illustrated p. 668.

71. Ibid., p. 668.

72. Ibid.

73. Ibid., p. 670.

74. Regina Soria, *Elihu Vedder: American Visionary Artist in Rome (1836–1923)* (Rutherford, N.J.: Fairleigh Dickinson University Press, 1970), p. 138.

75. Ibid., p. 139.

76. Ibid.

77. William Mackay Laffan, "The Tile Club," *Harper's Weekly*, 24 (January 31 1880), p. 75.

78. Ibid.

79. Ibid.

80. Ibid.

81. William Mackay Laffan, "The Tile Club Ashore," *The Century Magazine*, XXIII, No. 4 (February 1882), pp. 481–498.

82. Ibid., p. 481.

83. Ibid., p. 482.

84. Ibid.

85. Ibid.

86. Ibid., p. 481.

87. Aside from the fact that the personal lives of several participating artists do not conform with the dating of the summer trip in 1881, illustrations in the article are dated both 1880 and 1881. See Arthur Quartley, *The Bow of the Two Sisters*, July '80 (p. 486) and Quartley's *A Corner by the [Port Jefferson] Harbor*, 1881 (p. 495).

88. Ibid., p. 482.

89. Ibid., p. 483.

90. *New York Tribune*, July 18, 1887; information provided by Joseph Ditta, New-York Historical Society, Library Reference Department, N.Y.

91. Laffan, p. 484.

92. Ibid., p. 487.

93. Ibid., pp. 491–492.

94. Ibid., p. 493.

95. Ibid., p. 494.

96. Ibid., p. 495.

97. Ibid.

98. Lucas, p. 98.

99. Ibid., p. 115.

100. Ibid.

101. "An Extraordinary Symposium," *New York Times* (October 8, 1881), 5:4.

102. Lucas, p. 116.

103. Laffan, p. 496.

104. Ibid, p. 495.

105. Ibid, p. 497.

106. Ibid, p. 498.

107. Ibid.

108. Ibid.

109. Ibid.

110. For a full discussion of Vedder's work in the decorative arts at this time, see Soria, pp. 151–152.

111. Soria, pp. 171–172.

112. Annual proceedings and report of the St. Botolph Club, 1880.

113. Ibid.

114. "Catalogue of Pictures by the Tile Club, Exhibited at the St. Botolph Club," Boston, February 25, 1882. A brief notice of this exhibition appeared in *The New York Times* (March 6, 1882), 3:4.

115. Frank D. Millet, "Some American Tiles," *The Century Magazine*, XXIII, No. 6 (April, 1882), pp. 896–904.

116. Smith and Strahan, *A Book of the Tile Club*, p. 17.

117. Ibid., p. 1.

118. Ibid., p. 2.

119. The two buildings were purchased by David Maitland Armstrong and joined together for his use. In 1987 they were purchased by the Alexander Onassis Foundation and bequeathed to New York University as the "Center for Hellenic Studies." See: Hamilton Fish Armstrong, *Those Days* (New York: Harper & Row, 1963); and Scott Marshall, "The Greenwich Society for Historic Preservation," 1991 – brochure provided by Annette Blaugrund.

120. "The Tile Club Abroad," *Harper's Weekly* (November 23, 1882), p. 747.

121. Ibid., p. 748.

122. Ibid., p. 747.

123. Soria, p. 172.

124. *Harper's Christmas*, New York, December, 1882.

125. Soria, p. 157.

126. *L'Art*, Vol. 25, 1881, Septième Année, p. 170. This reference, as well as the one following, was brought to my attention by Bruce Weber.

127. *The Complete Letters of Vincent van Gogh*, (Greenwich, Conn.: New York Graphics Society, 1958), Vol. II, Letter No. 277, p. 20.

128. Ibid.

129. Ibid.

130. Soria, p. 172.

131. Ibid., p. 173.

132. See: "In Support of Liberty: European Paintings at the 1883 Pedestal Fund Art Loan Exhibition," (Southampton, N.Y.: The Parrish Art Museum, 1986), organized by Maureen C. O'Brien.

133. Soria, p. 177.

134. Soria, p. 178.

135. Soria, p. 180.

136. Soria, p. 178

137. Soria, p. 177.

138. "Rich Treasures of Art, Mr. W. T. Walters' Galleries, Viewed by a Distinguished Throng," *Baltimore Sun* (February 27 1884). The unpaginated clipping of this article was brought to my attention by William R. Johnston, who also pointed out the specific importance of Rousseau's painting.

139. "Glimpses of the Tile Club," *Art Amateur* (October 1884), p. 97–100.

140. Soria, p. 181.

141. For a full discussion of this see: Ronald G. Pisano, *William Merritt Chase (1849–1916): A Leading Spirit in American Art* (Seattle: Henry Art Gallery, University of Washington, 1983), pp. 77–82.

142. Smith and Strahan, *A Book of the Tile Club*, p. 105.

143. Ibid.

144. See William H. Gerdts, "The Square Format and Proto-Modernism in American Painting," *Arts Magazine* 50 (June 1976), pp. 70–75.

145. Smith and Strahan, *A Book of the Tile Club*, pp. 14, 17.

1. In one of his lectures on the decorative arts, William Morris remarked *Now all nations, however barbarous have made pottery . . . but none have ever failed to make it on true principles, none have ever made shapes ugly or base until quite modern times. I should say that the making of ugly pottery was one of the most remarkable inventions of our civilization.* Quoted from Richard and Hilary Myers, *William Morris Tiles* (Somerset, England: Richard Dennis, 1966), p. 11.

2. For a full discussion of English tile making, see Brian and Jill Austwick, *The Decorated Tile: An Illustrated History of English Tile-Making and Design* (London: Pitman House, 1980), Elisabeth Aslin, "Tiles in the Nineteenth Century," in Jon Catleugh, *William de Morgan Tiles* (Somerset, England: Richard Dennis, 1983), and Tony Herbert and Kathryn Huggins, *The Decorative Tile* (London: Phaidon Press, Ltd., 1995).

3. An encaustic tile was made by impressing a design upon a red quarry tile with a stamp and filling the resulting cavity with whitish clay, a process described in John Gough Nichols, *Examples of Decorative Tiles, Sometimes Termed Encaustic* (London: J. B. Nichols & Son, 1845), a book of specimens of medieval flooring tiles engraved after surviving originals. A surprising number of similar books appeared on this topic during the 1840s, including Owen Jones, *Examples of Encaustic Tiles, Drawn on Stone* (London: 1844).

4. Lewis F. Day (1845–1910), an English designer who worked for a number of tile companies as well as an author of many books on decorative motifs and design topics, reported that Jones's book, intending to replace "received forms . . . enfeebled by constant repetition" was a virtual guide for "floundering" manufacturers, decorators, and designers. See Lewis F. Day, "Victorian Progress in Applied Design," *Art Journal*, October 1887, pp. 187–88.

5. For full references on Christopher Dresser, see Catherine H. Voorsanger, "Dictionary of Architects, Artisans, Artists and Manufacturers," Doreen Bolger Burke et al., *In Pursuit of Beauty* (New York: Metropolitan Museum of Art, and Rizzoli, 1986), pp. 421–23.

6. John Ruskin, Lecture III, "Modern Manufacture and Design," *The Two Paths* (Reprint London and Toronto: J. M. Dent, 1919), pp. 136–37. Ruskin went on to decry the current fashion for room decoration in "flat patterns" and "dead colours," this part of his essay apparently ignored by the "pattern makers" of the period. *The Two Paths* went through nineteen printings in America between 1859, when it first appeared, and 1891.

7. The initial prospectus for the Morris firm stated: "The growth of Decorative Art in this country . . . has now reached a point at which it seems that artists of reputation should devote their time to it." Quoted in Lionel Lambourne, *The Aesthetic Movement* (London: Phaidon Press, Ltd., 1996), p. 18.

8. Oscar Wilde was also a devotee of blue and white Oriental porcelains as were the two most important art patrons in late-nineteenth-century London, Frederick Leyland and Albert Ionides. Whistler's spectacular fallout with his patron Leyland concerned changes to the program for the famed Peacock Room, designed to accommodate Leyland's collection of porcelain. In 1884, Frederick Miller published a series of articles on pottery and glass painting in *Furniture Gazette*, in which he expressed a preference for hand-painted tiles over printed ones; elsewhere he discussed the spontaneity of Oriental ceramics, opining that the painters of such pottery were true artists. *Furniture Gazette* 21 (January 1884), p. 18.

9. Quoted from Minton, Hollins & Co. Trade Catalogue in *Minton's Tiles: 1835–1935* (Stoke-on-Trent, England: Stoke-on-Trent Museum and Art Gallery, 1984), p. 14. The only designers known at Minton, Hollins & Co. were Albert Slater, W. P. Simpson, and John Moyr Smith, who worked for both Minton's firms.

10. Annamarie Stapleton, "John Moyr Smith 1839–1912," *Journal of the Decorative Arts Society* 20 (1996), pp. 18–29. Moyr Smith worked for W. B. Simpson & Sons, who provided tiles for the Boston house of Mrs. Charles Joy, the interiors of which were illustrated in the *American Architect and Building News* in 1876. I would like to thank Annamarie Stapleton for her help with this project.

11. Doulton's produced mainly pottery, but exquisite painted tiles were made for use as fire surrounds and as inset panels for the simplified rectilinear furniture of the period.

12. Of the three refreshment rooms, Morris, Marshall, Faulkner & Co. were given the West Dining Room, in which

not a single tile, but for the flooring, is to be found. The entire room was finished in a variety of gilded, painted, and embossed techniques. The museum's own design team under James Gamble did the larger center room, and in it virtually every surface is covered by solid, patterned, or painted majolica Minton's tiles. Even the necessary supporting columns were sheathed in tiles, which caused some controversy at the time over the appropriate use of ceramic tiles to sheath a structural element. Euridice, Sappho, Medea, Europa, Proserpine, Andromeda, Venus, Helen, Rhodopsis, and Oenone are the female figures portrayed in the Grill Room. It should also be noted that much of the now-lost interior decoration of the South Kensington museum was tiled, and that the Museum actively collected the "industrial arts" of its time.

13. Professor Walter Smith, *The Masterpieces of the Centennial International Exhibition Illustrated, Vol II., Industrial Art* (Philadelphia: Gebbie & Barrie, 1876). p. 385.

14. Jennie J. Young, *The Ceramic Art* (New York: Harper & Brothers, 1879), pp. 368–69. It should be noted that the author of this book apparently knew Tile Club member George Boughton "of London" well enough to know that he had a plate with an image entitled "At Montreal," designed by John M. Falconer of Greenpoint porcelain in Brooklyn. See p. 486.

15. Ibid., p. 372.

16. Smith, *The Masterpieces of the Centennial Exhibition*, Vol. II, pp. 418–19.

17. Millet wrote "Some American Tiles" in 1883 for the *Century Illustrated Monthly Magazine* (formerly *Scribner's Monthly*), which described the tile works of J. and J. G. Low in Boston. Between 1875 and 1877, *Scribner's* published a series of articles by Clarence Cook, the leading proponent of Aesthetic movement household decoration in America. One page illustrated a simple wooden fire surround inset with tiles, captioned "He Can Do Little Who Can't Do This." See Clarence Cook, "Beds and Tables, Stools and Candlesticks, VI," *Scribner's* 12 (May–October 1876), p. 805.

18. I would like to thank Alice Cooney Frelinghuysen for discussing with me Cottier's activity as a tile painter (Scholarship Files, Metropolitan Museum of Art). I would also like to thank Max Kolbe Donnelly for sharing with me his recent work on Cottier. See Max Kolbe Donnelly, *Cottier & Co. (1864–1915): Establishing a Context for the Second Glasgow School* (Sotheby's Institute, London: unpublished dissertation, 1998).

19. George Warrin, Edward Lycett, and Bennett and White all advertised themselves as pottery painters. Mr. Warrin of "Warrin & Lycett" was said to have had fifteen years experience as a decorator of pottery. See Young, *The Ceramic Art*, p. 483. Edward Lycett was an Englishman known for his decorated tableware and china in the French styles. John Bennet was another English pottery painter who was briefly associated with Lycett. Full references can be found in Voorsanger, "Dictionary," Burke et al., *In Pursuit of Beauty*, pp. 426–27. The activity of Doulton's John Bennett is discussed in Alice Cooney Frelinghuysen, "Aesthetic Forms in Ceramics and Glass," in Burke et al., *In Pursuit of Beauty*, pp. 217–19.

20. Quoted in Frelinghuysen, "Aesthetic Forms," Burke et al., *In Pursuit of Beauty*, p. 220.

21. "American Girls as Decorators," *Crockery and Glass Journal*, Vol. 6, No. 20 (November 22, 1877), p. 14. This article also reported that in London, women had become house decorators, the sisters of a "well known literary man" taking "the entire arrangement and adornment of the house in their charge."

22. *Crockery and Glass Journal*, Vol. 7, No. 16 (April 18, 1878), p. 28.

23. Ibid.

1. Thomas L. Haskell, "The Culture of Professionalism," *The New York Review of Books* (13 October 1977), pp. 28–33.

2. Mary Alice Mackay, "Sketch Club Drawings for Byron's 'Darkness' and Scott's 'Lay of the Last Minstrel'," *Master Drawings* (Summer, 1997), p. 142.

3. Minutes of the Sketch Club, Century Association Papers, Archives of American Art, Washington, D. C.

4. Minutes of the Sketch Club.

5. Ibid.

6. Frank Mather, *The Century*, New York, Century Association, 1947, p. 159

7. Louis Lang, "Art History of the Century Association from 1847–1880," unpublished manuscript, Archives of American Art, Washington, D. C., lists all works of art exhibited at Century from November 6, 1869–December 4, 1880.

8. Jervis McEntee Diaries, Archives of American Art, Washington, D.C.

9. Linda H. Skalet, *The Market for American Painting in New York: 1870–1915* (Ph. D. dissertation, Johns Hopkins University, 1980), pp. 250–286 list Gentlemen's Clubs Exhibitions in New York for the period.

10. Francis Gerry Fairfield, *The Clubs of New York* (New York, Henry L. Hinton, 1873), pp. 271–272.

11. Ibid., pp. 272–273.

12. William H. Bishop, "Young Artist's Life in New York," *Scribner's Monthly* (January 1880), p. 360.

13. William H. Shelton, *The Salmagundi Club: A History* (Boston: Houghton Mifflin, 1918), pp. 21–22, 27, and Salmagundi Club Papers, Archives of American Art, Washington, D. C.

14. Low's drawing appeared in *Scribner's Monthly* (January 1880), p. 360.

15. Shelton, *The Salmagundi Club*, p. 16.

16. Unidentified clipping, dated 15 November 1888, Salmagundi Club Papers.

17. Shelton, *The Salmagundi Club*, p. 50.

18. Ibid., pp. 71–72.

19. "Studio Life in New York," *The Art Journal*, Vol. 5, 1879, p. 343.

20. Nym Crinkle, "Round About the Kit Kat," *Quarterly Illustrator*, Vol. 2, 1894, p. 364.

21. See Constance Koppelman, *Nature in Art and Culture: The Tile Club* (Ph. D. Dissertation, State University of New York, Stony Brook, 1985), pp. 81–88 and Albert Parry, *Garrets and Pretenders: A History of Bohemianism in America* (New York: Dover Publications, 1960), for a more complete discussion of the Bohemian phenomenon.

22. Crinkle, "Round About the Kit Kat," pp. 364–365.

23. Ralph Fabri, *History of the American Watercolor Society: The First Hundred Years* (New York, American Watercolor Society, 1964); p. 12 quotes the minutes of the first meeting.

24. Fabri, *History of the American Watercolor Society*, p. 15 quotes letter of May 15, 1868.

25. "The Society of Decorative Arts," *Scribner's Monthly*, September 1881, p. 701 and Karal Ann Marling, "Portrait of the Artist as a Young Woman: Miss Dora Wheeler," *Bulletin of the Cleveland Museum of Art*, February 1978, p. 50 discusses Candace Wheeler's campaign to have her daughter's needlework designs recognized as true works of art.

26. Society of Decorative Arts, "First Annual Report of the Society of Decorative Arts of the City of New York," January 1, 1878, p. 61, and "Second Annual Report of the Society of Decorative Arts of the City of New York," January 1, 1879, pp. 24–25.

27. Society of Decorative Arts, "Second Annual Report," pp. 19–20.

28. Ripley Hitchkock, *Etching in America*, New York, (White, Stokes and Allen, 1886), p. iii.

APPENDIX

Members of the Tile Club and their known sobriquets

Edwin Austin ABBEY (1852–1911) – *Chestnut* (refers to Abbey's telling of old stories)

William C. BAIRD Honorary – *Barytone* (famous baritone singer)

George Henry BOUGHTON (1834–1905) Honorary – *Puritan* (known for his paintings of Puritans)

William Gedney BUNCE (1840–1916) – *Bishop*

Charles Green BUSH (1842–1909) – *Scratch* (illustrator)

William Merritt CHASE (1849–1916) – *Briareus* (one of the hundred-handed sons of Mother Earth in Greek mythology)

Frederick DIELMAN (1847–1935) – *Terrapin* (because Dielman was from Baltimore, home of turtle soup)

Alexander W. DRAKE (1843–1916)

Arthur B. FROST (1851–1928) – *Icicle* (play off his surname)

R. Swain GIFFORD (1840–1905) – *Griffin* (another rendition of his surname)

Winslow HOMER (1836–1910) – *Obtuse Bard* (perhaps reference to his personality)

Antonio KNAUTH Honorary – *Horsehair* (perhaps referring to his playing the cello)

Gustave KOBBÉ (1857–1918) Honorary – *Husk*

William Mackay LAFFAN (1848–1909) – *Polyphemus* (a cyclops – Laffan had one eye, the other of glass)

Dr. J. LEWENBERG Honorary – *Catgut* (referring to the strings of a violin which he played)

George W. MAYNARD (1843–1923) – *Bird of Freedom*

Francis D. MILLET (1846–1912) – *Bulgarian* (well known as a correspondent for the Russo-Turkish war)

William R. O'DONOVAN (1844–1920) – *O'Donoghue* (variation of his surname)

Walter PARIS (1842–1906) – *Gaul* (play on words referring to his surname)

Alfred PARSONS (1830–1920) Honorary – *Burr* or *Englishman*

William Agnew PATON (1848–1918) – *Haggis*

Arthur QUARTLEY (1839–1886) – *Marine* (his speciality was marine paintings)

Charles S. REINHART (1844–1896) – *Sirius*

Augustus SAINT-GAUDENS (1848–1907) – *Saint* (based on his surname)

Napoleon SARONY (1821–1896) – *Hawk*

Earl SHINN (1837–1886) – *Bone* (likely a play off his surname)

Niromichi SHUGIO – *Varnish*

F. Hopkinson SMITH (1838–1915) – *Owl*

Charles TRUSLOW Honorary – *Boarder*

John H. TWACHTMAN (1853–1902) – *Pie*

Elihu VEDDER (1836–1923) – *Pagan* (perhaps referring to Rome, Italy, where he lived)

J. Alden WEIR (1852–1919) – *Cadmium* (he was partial to using cadmium yellow in his paintings)

Stanford WHITE (1853–1906) – *Beaver* (probably because of his busy lifestyle)

Edward WIMBRIDGE – *Grasshopper*

SELECTED BIBLIOGRAPHY

In addition to sources included in the notes

Baury, Louis. "The Story of the Tile Club," *Bookman* 35 (June 1912), pp. 381–396.

Braff, Phyllis. "Artists and East Hampton," exhibition catalogue (East Hampton: Guild Hall, August 14–October 3, 1976).

Buel, Clarence C. "Log of an Ocean Studio," *The Century Magazine* 27, No. 3 (January 1884), pp. 356–371.

Burke, Doreen Bolger. *J. Alden Weir: An American Impresionist* (Newark: University of Delaware Press, 1983).

de Kay, Charles. *Bohemia, A Tragedy of Modern Life* (New York: Scribner's, 1878).

Gerdts, William H. "The Square Format and Proto-Modernism in American Paintings," *Arts Magazine* 50 (June 1976), pp. 70–75.

Kenin, Richard. *Return to Albion: Americans in England (1760-1940)* (New York: Reinhart and Winston, 1979).

Millet, J. B. "The Tile Club," *Julian Alden Weir: An Appreciation of His Life and Works*, (New York: E. P. Dutton & Co., 1922).

Moran, Ruth. "Notes on the Tile Club," unpublished manuscript, Pennypacker, L.I., Collection East Hampton Free Library (East Hampton, NY: undated).

"Our Art Clubs. IV. – The Tile Club." *The Art Union*, Vol. 2, No. 5 (November 1885), p. 97.

Pisano, Ronald G. "The Tile Club and the Development of Plein Air Painting in America," *American Artist* (April 1998), pp. 54–61, 81–82.

Rattray, Jeanette Edwards. *East Hampton a History: Geneaologies of Early Families* (New York: Country Life Press, 1953).

"Retrospective Exhibition from the Work of the Tile Club and Their Followers, who First Discovered the Picturesque Qualities of East Hampton," exhibition catalogue (East Hampton: Guild Hall, August 19–September 1, 1931).

Rubin, Ronnie. "The Tile Club, 1877–1887," (M. A. thesis, New York University, 1967).

Saint-Gaudens, Augustus. *The Reminiscences of Augustus Saint-Gaudens*, edited and amplified by Homer Saint-Gaudens (New York: The Century Co., 1913), 2 Vols.

Sharpey-Schafer, Joyce A. *Soldier of Fortune* (Utica, NY: 1984).

Shelton, William Henry. "Artists Life in New York in the Days of Oliver Horn," *Critic* 43 (July 1903), pp. 31–40.

Shelton, William Henry. *The Salmagundi Club* (New York: Houghton Mifflin & Co., 1918).

"The Tile Club at Whitehall/A Cordial Reception – The Club's Canal-Boat-Some of the Work Done," *New York Times* (July 10, 1879), 5:4.

Young, Dorothy Weir. *The Life and Letters of J. Alden Weir* (New Haven: Yale University Press, 1960).

Young, Mahonri Sharp. "The Tile Club Revisited," *The American Art Journal* 2 (Fall 1970), pp. 81–91.

ACKNOWLEDGMENTS

Among those to whom I am particularly indebted are the many private collectors, commercial art galleries and museums who have so generously allowed me to reproduce their works of art in this book, and who have been credited in the appropriate captions. Additionally, the following private collectors have offered invaluable assistance: Arthur G. Altschul, Karen H. Bechtel, David Kiehl, Gustavus Remak Ramsay and, especially, Graham D. Williford. Art dealers and auction house personnel who have been helpful in lending their extensive expertise include: James Berry-Hill, Alex Boyle, Lillian Brenwasser, Vivian Bullaudy, Mildred Thaler Cohen, Jeff Cooley, Stuart Feld, Martha Fleischman, Debra Force, Karen Michelle Guido, Fred Hill, Ramona Hillier, Vance Jordon, Betty Krulik, Jill Newhouse, Suzanne Perrault, Andrew Schoelkopf, Edward Shein, Ira Spanierman, John H. Surovek, and Lois Wagner. Among the other scholars in the field, museum professionals and those who have offered very special advice, I would like to express my gratitude to: Linda Ayres, Annette Blaugrund, Jonathon Boos, Jeffrey Boys, Phyllis Braff, Charles Burlingham, David Cassedy, Kate Cameron, Hildegard Cummings, Gail S. Davidson, David Dearinger, Ann Cohen DePietro, Joseph Ditta, Joel and Patty Dryer, John Dryfhout, Peter H. Falk, Linda Ferber, Ruth Fine, Dorothy King, Ken Fitch, Tom Folk, Barbara Gallati, Abigail Booth Gerdts, William H. Gerdts, Mary Anne Goley, Helen Harrison, Jan Inners, William R. Johnston, Alexander Katlan, Joy Ketsenbaum, Henry Korn, Elizabeth Kornhauser, Richard C. Kugler, Alicia Longwell, Don McIver, Ken Maddox, Anne Markham, Clark Marlor, J. Bradford Millet, Lucy Oakley, Lisa Panzera, Lisa Peters, Dawn Pheysey, Dianne Pilgrim, Henry Reed, Beverly Rood, Inger Schoelkopf, Paul Schweizer, Ray V. J. Scrag, Ray Smith, Patrick Sowle, Donna Stein, Stephen Van Dyk, Roberta Waddell, Ed Watkins, Bruce Weber, H. Barbara Weinberg, and Claire White. Special mention should be made of my co-authors who have provided insightful auxiliary essays, Linda Skalet and Mary Ann Apicella.

I am especially pleased to have worked on this book with the most able staff at Abrams, Elaine Stainton, who edited my text, Julia Gaviria, and Judy Hudson. The book has been published in conjunction with the traveling exhibition *The Tile Club and the Aesthetic Movement in America: 1877–1887* arranged by The Museums at Stony Brook, Stony Brook, New York. I am grateful for having been given the opportunity to guest curate the exhibition, and in this capacity would like to thank William Ayres, chief curator, who arranged to have the book published at Abrams, Joshua Ruff, who greatly assisted in logistical arrangements for the exhibition and book, and Ita Berkow who collaborated with me in the early stages of this venture. It must be noted that major funding for the exhibition was provided by The Henry Luce Foundation, with additional funding by The New York State Council on the Arts, The Simons Foundation, and The Cowles Charitable Trust. Furthermore I must thank Deborah J. Johnson, President of The Museums of Stony Brook for her support and confidence in the worthiness of this project and for her special work, with the assistance of Amanda Meyers, in raising the funds necessary for its fruition.

Finally, and foremost, I am grateful for the extensive efforts, and perseverance, of my colleague, D. Frederick Baker, who ably assisted me in every step of this publication and exhibition. Without his unselfish and very considerable labor, it would never have been possible.

Ronald G. Pisano
New York

INDEX

PHOTOGRAPH CREDITS

Lyman Allyn Art Museum, New London, CT: 10; Collection Arthur G. Altschul, New York, NY: 28; American Academy of Arts and Letters, New York, NY: 65 (top); Archives of American Art, Washington, DC: 34; Baker/Pisano Collection: 41 (top), 44 (bottom); Collection Karen H. Bechtel: 25; Blairman & Son, London, England: 76 (top); Brooklyn Museum of Art, Brooklyn, NY: 24 (bottom); The Century Association, New York, NY: 12 (top), 58, 84; Cincinnati Art Museum, Cincinnati, OH: 33 (top); University of Cincinnati Fine Arts Collection, Cincinnati, OH: 54; Collearn House Hotel, Auchterarder, Scotland: 74, 75; Cooley Gallery, Old Lyme, CT: 36; Corcoran Gallery of Art, Washington, DC: 57; East Hampton Free Library, East Hampton, NY: 31; The Fine Art Society, London, England: 71 (bottom), 73 (top), 78; Thomas Goode, London, England: 77; Guild Hall Museum, East Hampton, NY: 8, 9, 21, 22 (top), 23; Haslam & Whiteway, Ltd., London, England: 68, 70, 71 (top), 72, 73 (bottom), 76 (bottom), 80 (bottom); Hudson River Museum, Yonkers, NY: 82; Vance Jordan Gallery, New York, NY: 52 (top); Joslyn Art Museum, Omaha, NE: 61; Kennedy Galleries, New York, NY: 49 (bottom); Collection Janet Lehr: 92; Leven Collection: 62; Lightfoot Collection: 32 (bottom); Collection Mr. and Mrs. John F. McGuigan: 24 (top); Metropolitan Museum of Art, New York, NY: 65; National Academy of Design, New York, NY: 13 (top), 33 (bottom); National Portrait Gallery, Washington, DC: 49 (top), 64; New-York Historical Society, New York, NY: 13; Old Dartmouth Historical Society, New Bedford, MA: 93; Prints Division, New York Public Library, New York, NY: 30 (top); Pennsylvania Academy of the Fine Arts, Philadelphia, PA: 42; Philadelphia Museum of Art. John G. Johnson Collection: 51; Portland Art Museum, Portland, OR: 47 (bottom); Private Collections: 16, 17, 20, 22 (bottom), 26, 29, 32 (top), 35, 37 (bottom), 38, 39, 41 (bottom), 44 (top), 45, 47 (top), 53 (top), 59, 60; The Salmagundi Club, New York, NY: 89, 91; The Springfield Museums, Springfield, MA: 27; Victoria and Albert Museum, London, England: 80 (top); Wadsworth Atheneum, Hartford, CT: 55, 56; Whaling Museum, New Bedford, MA: 37 (top); Collection Graham D. Williford: 18,19, 30 (bottom), 43, 46, 53 (bottom), 63; Yale University Art Museum, New Haven, CT: 86.